NAVY TIN
CAN MAN

NAVY TIN CAN MAN

CAPT R.A. JAYCOX

iUniverse, Inc.
Bloomington

NAVY TIN CAN MAN

iUniverse books may be ordered through booksellers or by contacting:

iUniverse
1663 Liberty Drive
Bloomington, IN 47403
www.iuniverse.com
1-800-Authors (1-800-288-4677)

ISBN: 978-1-4620-2821-4 (sc)
ISBN: 978-1-4620-2822-1 (ebk)

Printed in the United States of America

iUniverse rev. date: 06/23/2011

ABOUT THE BOOKS COVER IT PICTURES THE USS MAYRANT DD—402 AND THE SHIPS CREW

Following the success of the north African invasion *Mayrant* spent several months on convoy duty off the east coast, returning to north African waters in May. Passing through the Straits of Gibraltar. she arrived Mers-el Kebir, 23 May. Throughout June she cruised the north African coast from Oran to Bizerte, escorting convoys and conducting antisubmarine patrols. On 14 July, she shifted her base of operations north toward to Sicily. While on antiair patrol off Palermo, 26 July, she was attacked by Luftwaffe dive bombers.

A near miss, only a yard or two off her port bow, during this encounter caused extensive damage. Her side ruptured and her engineering space flooded, she was towed into Palermo with five dead and 18 wounded.

In spite of her damage, the destroyer's guns helped repel several Luftwaffe raids on Palermo the next week. On 9 August, she was towed to Malta where temporary repairs were completed by 14 November. She then steamed to Charleston, S.C. for extensive yard repairs.

Back in fighting trim 15 May 1944 she departed Charleston for Casco Bay, Maine. For the next year she operated primarily along the east coast, escorting new cruisers and carriers on shakedown and protecting coastal convoys. During this year she also escorted two convoys to the Mediterranean.

On patrol off New England, 5 April 1945, *Mayrant* went to the rescue of the cargo ship *Atlantic States*, torpedoed off Cape Cod Light. Despite heavy weather, the destroyer transferred members of her crew to the powerless merchantman and took her in tow. For 2 days, until oceangoing tugs had her under control, they battled waves and breaking lines to keep Atlantic States from drifting and sinking.

The war in Europe drawing to a close, *Mayrant* transferred to the Pacific Fleet. She arrived Pearl Harbor 21 May and underwent intensive training in shore bombardment and night operations. On 2 June she sailed for Ulithi escorting convoys to Iwo Jima, Okinawa, and Saipan. After the end of hostilities, *Mayrant* was designated to make preliminary arrangements for the surrender of the enemy garrison on Marcus, a bypassed island in the central Pacific. With the official surrender of the island 31 August, the destroyer took up air-sea rescue operations in the Marshalls and Marianas.

On 30 December, *Mayrant* arrived at San Diego for a brief stay before heading back to the central Pacific. Designated as test ship for operation "Crossroads," the 1946 atomic bomb tests, she arrived Bikini Atoll, Marshall Islands, 31 May 1946. Surviving the tests, but too highly contaminated, *Mayrant* decommissioned at Bikini 28 August 1946. She was destroyed 4 April 1948 and struck from the Navy Register on the 30th.

Mayrant received three battle stars for World War II service.

INTRODUCTION

THE SEA HATH NO KING BUT GOD ALONE

DANTE GABRIEL ROSETTI

Today the alarm clock rang with its usual morning greeting. It buzzed at 4:30 a.m., even though I was awake at 4:00. My daily routine started. Virginia, my wife, was still sleeping, so I went out to the kitchen to look out at the flag in my backyard to see how the wind was. It was a light wind. Great! The walleyes will be hungry, I hope. I went to my computer to check the forecast. The advisory told me that the wind was coming from the southwest at 10 to 15 knots, going to 10 to 20 tonight. I put the coffee water on, turned on the television to wake up my wife, and swallowed a couple of pain pills for my back. I got dressed, then sat down to tie my shoes, and my back screamed, "Hello! Good morning! Why did you get me up so early? You know that you're 81-years-old. Go back to bed!"

I had a walleye charter at 6:00 a.m. with six guys from Columbus, Ohio. Virginia got up and made coffee. I grabbed my cell phone, a cup of coffee, and a donut. I was on my way. The morning air smelled great! The sky was clear, and the sun was trying to come up over the eastern sky. I took a block of ice from my freezer in the garage, and jumped in my pickup. It was a 4-minute drive to the dock at Spitzer's Marina, here in Lorain. On my way, I stopped off at Mc Donald's to get a sausage biscuit at the drive-in. From there, I drove down to the dock. As I came down the hill to the parking area, I looked at the lake, and discovered that the wind was coming from the northeast and blowing. Damn those weather guys! After I parked the truck, I bumped into my good friend, Frank Katrick, captain of the *Y-Knot* charter boat. I walked down to my 31-feet-long, twin diesel Tiara, after I unlocked the gate to Dock C. Once I opened the captain's door and put on the deck lights, I began my usual pre-charter duties: grabbed the engine keys, put them in the ignition, opened the engine hatch to check the oil and cooling water, as well as inspected the oil level in the gears and engine. Everything was ship-shape, so I closed the hatch and started the engines. This sky was starting to lighten up, and the wind shifted more to north.

The guys of the fishing charter arrived and were laughing and happy as most charter guys are when they get a chance to go fishing. As they piled into the boat, I greeted them all by name because they had been with me before. Once they were situated, I briefed them on the safety rules—life jackets, etc. They howled when I asked them if the pointy end of the boat went first, and wondered what the hell kind of captain they had steering the boat. I hooked up the engines to 3,000 rpms, and we were off to the fishing grounds. The walleyes were in big trouble today, I thought, and wished that the lake would calm down a bit. After all of these years I still do not enjoy rough weather, but if the fish were biting, I won't even notice.

We were underway after I untied the dock lines and unhooked the shore power. As the sun was just making its way over the eastern sky, we passed the Lorain lighthouse, clearing the harbor. My diesel engines were purring like kittens when I hooked up to 1500 rpms. After we cleared the outer light, I set a course of 330 degrees. We ran out to the 32 line about 3.5 miles when I slowed the boat to get ready to set out our fishing lines. After that, I set a course for 165 degrees east, and then I shut one engine down to slow to two and a half miles per hour. I put out "bag" to slow us even further to two mph.

We got our rods down from the holders and baited our worm harnesses with night crawlers. We are running 30 jet on our board lines, and we have three lines on each side. The first line out is set to 150 feet; the second line out is set at 120 feet, and the third line is set out at 100 feet.

We no more than got the lines out, when I heard, "FISH ON!" Number 3 board line pulled out of the clip, and away went the line screaming. I hollered, "Steelhead!" and the boat came alive. Out of the water at about 150 feet back, the water erupted, and the nice steelhead continuously jumped. I grabbed the rod, let the line run, and handed it to a customer. The smile on his face is worth a "high five." The "Steely" finally got tired. We brought him in and netted a nice 27 inch fish. Immediately thereafter the rods were all starting to catch walleyes. Our fish box was beginning to fill up with the fish after two hours, and it was only 8:00 a.m.

With six fishermen on board, we needed only five more fish to make our limit of thirty-six. The fish averaged about 3—to 4-pounds each, so that we had about one hundred pounds of walleyes by 8:30. I asked the guys if they wanted to go for perch because it was still early. They said no, "We have our fish; let's go in." So we pulled the lines and planer boards, plus the "bag" and headed for port. We had covered about four miles of water and limited out in two and a half hours. Fantastic fishing! All of the guys on the boat were happy as we headed back to Lorain Harbor. This was not an unusual trip, as fishing this year out of Lorain was outstanding, with limits after limits. Sometimes it takes two hours to limit out, while other times it took six or seven, but it is a fun thing because these walleyes are delicious. We reached the lighthouse and slowed down as we entered the harbor.

The passengers complained, then laughed, "We didn't even have time to eat our lunch." I asked them if they wanted to anchor and to eat, to which they agreed. So I shut the engines down, and they broke out their beer and food. We sat there enjoying the day and talked. I told them some stories about my Navy days, and one guy let me know that he was a P-51 pilot in the 8th Air Force during World War II. We hit it off right away, because I loved that airplane. What a beautiful sight to see those guys take off and fly from Iwo Jima!

We finished talking and eating before I pulled anchor and headed for the dock. The guys wanted to take pictures of their fish, so the crew and I hung the fish on a board with hooks on it. They snapped some pictures. It was about noon when they paid me, and we helped them to get their fish in their coolers. I gave them directions on how to get to Artic Seafood to clean their fish before they left.

We cleaned the boat with a pressure washer which does a great job, and I checked out the engines and fuel gauges, so that I was set for tomorrow when we have a perch trip. The final chore was to check the dock lines and to lock up the cabin.

My friend, Ken, my crew, and I then went up to the restaurant to have lunch. It was only 1:00, so I called my wife, Virginia, to meet us at Chris's for lunch. Of course, she jumped at the chance to go to a restaurant and enjoy a nice lunch. My back was killing me from a nerve that was pinched. At 81, I figure it is part of the game, and tried to ignore it. We finished eating and I bade Ken farewell until the next morning. My wife and I headed home.

As I walked into the house, my wife informed me that the sink drain was leaking. I groaned and lay down on the kitchen floor to check it out. Sure enough, the drain had come loose, so I put it back in place and tightened it up. After that chore was finished, Virginia told me that the garbage man was coming today, which means, "Take the garbage out!" I groaned again, and wished that I had spent more time fishing today.

As the day wore on, at 4:00, I grew pretty tired and wanted to lie down and rest. It was just as I was considering a nap when my wife asked to go out for supper. I groaned again, and said, "Yeah, sure." We drove out to Vermillion to the Ponderosa and enjoyed a nice supper. We left, and Virginia suggested, "Let's go to Big Lots and get a lounge chair for the backyard." Once again, I groaned and agreed, "But let's go home first."

At home, I jumped in the tub and was soaking the soreness out of my body when the little lady remembers that we had not mown the grass. I told her that it was dark and that I would get to it in the morning. I turned on the television to watch the Cleveland Indians lose, and it is 10:00, and I'm beat.

As I lay awake thinking of what my tomorrow might bring, it is also time to think of a lot of my yesterdays. Many of my charter patrons have told me that I should write a book about my life, because they enjoyed my stories so much. And so, here are eighty-one years of memories of a man who loves his boats and who loves the water.

Large Walleye Caught on the *Skipper—2*

My wife Virginia, with three nice perch.

My Dayton friends with Walleye and Steelhead

CHAPTER ONE - THE ROWBOAT

ONLY THE GUY WHO ISN'T ROWING HAS TIME TO
ROCK THE BOAT
                    JEAN PAUL SARTRE

My story starts on June 27, 1926 when I was born to Ruth and Plynn Jaycox of 1113 West Erie Avenue in Lorain Ohio. They called me Bobby, and I grew up in a close-knit family with my dad working at United States Steel, and my mom working part-time at Ruth's Tea Room downtown. We were not a rich family, but survived the ravages of the Depression Era.

I went to school at Irving, and my first grade teacher was one of the "E" sisters who carried a foot-long ruler and seemed to enjoy using it. This first grade introduction to school left a bad impression of how life was going to be in a classroom. Because of this, my interest in school was not good, so my fancies took on another course.

My grand dad, Tracy Coats, was a bootlegger in his spare time, making beer and wine, and trading it for fish from the tugs in Lorain. He worked full time as an engineer for Lake Terminal Railroad. As I grew up in the Depression years, money was pretty scarce, so with my mom and dad both working, there was little for me to do. I became very close to my grand dad. As I grew older, I helped him to cap beer bottles and to take care of the brew. My love for him became greater because he often came home from work with animals such has ground hogs, snakes, and young rabbits. He lived close by, so that my cousin, Bill Coats, and I used to visit and watch him make pets of these animals. At one time he had a ground hog that he had raised to be fairly big, so he had my cousin and me dig a hole in the backyard for the animal to enter to hibernate in for the winter. We dug for what seemed to be forever, and when we were finished, we watched every day to see if the groundhog used the hole that we made for him. Well, winter came, and we didn't see the animal anymore; we thought he was in our hole. As it turned out, he dug his own hole under the front porch which ended our ground hog hole digging days.

My grand dad loved to fish, and when he wasn't working or going out on the fish tugs, he let me come along to help row his boat out to the lighthouse to still fish. The boat, which had two sets of oar locks, moved along pretty quickly. We usually stopped at the lighthouse to get some minnows from the keeper. He was a jolly old guy who kept the bait in a homemade trap in the water for fishermen who came that way from time to time. He had a large pole that stuck out over the water, and it had a line with a big net which is how he caught the minnows. [Night fishing was a big thing in those days, and I can recall guys fishing off the break wall, putting their fish on a stringer and the minks who lived there used to grab the stringer and help themselves to a free meal.] After we got our bait from the lighthouse keeper, we rowed around the corner to my grand dad's favorite spot about twenty feet from the light. We had an old lantern from the railroad, and as it became dark, the minnows swarmed on the surface so that the white bass and Saugers came up to chase them. Our live bag was a burlap sack that we hung over the side of the boat. It didn't take long in those days to fill the bag with blue pike, Saugers, [We used to call them "sand pike."], white bass, perch, and walleyes. We sat there one night and caught fish as fast as we dropped a line. After about an hour, we knew that the bag had to be full, and when we pulled the bag up to go, we found the bag to be empty. It had a hole in it. As we put the fish in, they just swam out of the other end.

Once we returned to my grandfather's place, we put the fish on a large round table that he had made. It had a hole in the center in which he placed a bucket. He cleaned the fish there and dropped the guts in the bucket, along with the scales.

At that time of my life, my mother was sick and in the hospital recovering from tuberculosis. My dad was then a member of the fire department. The story of how he got the job is pretty interesting. You see, my dad was a staunch Republican, and he played baseball with Uncle Joe Uhali, who was head man with the Democrats. Because they were such good pals on the baseball field, Uhali helped my dad to get the position with the fire department.

Once I got my "feet wet," so to speak, going fishing with my grand dad, I became hooked on the lake. I spent much of my time on the beach, fishing, or just being there. When we moved to the East Side of Lorain, on Idaho Avenue, my dad used to spank me for going down to the lake, but I just turned right around, and off I went, like a rabbit in a briar patch, back down to the water. One time I bought a kayak from a kid for $10.00 and painted it green. I couldn't wait for it to dry and took it down to the lake where I paddled it all the way over to the lighthouse. By the time I returned home, I was covered with green paint. My ass hurt for a week after my dad got done with me, but the very next day, I went right back down to my beloved beach.

When I was around fourteen years old, I had a row boat, and there was a swimming race from Century Park to Lakeview Park. My dad and I rowed the boat while Tom Kane swam the entire course side stroke.

We moved back to the West Side to Second Street. My friends, there, were George Honashoski, Jack and Stubby Mittenbuller, the Maddens—Bud and Joe, and the Heiman brothers. There were others, but I don't remember their names. I used to hang around Hot Waters, fishing and enjoying the lake. Red's Boat House was there, which the Heimans later took over and ran a rental boat place. I became fascinated with boats by the time we moved up to West Erie Avenue, and I had naively built my first boat in the basement of my house. Why was I naïve? Well, I had to cut it in half to get it out of the cellar, and then had to rebuild it to use it.

As a teenager, I worked at odd jobs to make money, and bought a sailboat for $15. I hung around at Harmon's Beach at that time with "Shirt Tail" Kellaher, Art O'Hara, Bob Cromer, and guys who had Comet sailboats. Harmon's Beach at that time was covered with seaweed, and the water level was almost up to the side of the bank. We waded out for about sixty feet in four to five feet of water. We used to drive a pipe in the water and moor our boats to it. There had to be about 10 to 15 boats down there. The Comet Class sailboats were very popular, and some expert boat builders were in the area. Bob Cromer comes to mind as does Doesendong. I'm sure that I got the spelling wrong, but I recall going over to their barn and watching those guys build boats. They were artists with wood. As an aside, Cromer later served his war time in the Coast Guard.

CHAPTER TWO - THE SAILBOAT

FOR WHATEVER WE LOSE (LIKE A YOU OR
A ME),IT IS ALWAYS OUR SELF WE FIND IN
THE SEA.

E.E.CUMMINGS

Art O'Hara asked me one time to sail his boat for him. We entered race after race, and as the new kid on the block, I think the best we did was second place. Later Art told me that he wanted me to take the boat up to Put-In-Bay for the Nationals. God, I had not been out of Lorain, and I had no idea where this place was. I knew it was west, but had no inkling of how far west. I thought if I just headed in that direction, sooner or later, I would bump into it. So, I set sail and started out west—no compass and no charts—just native instincts.

The Comet sailboats have a centerboard that slides up and down to keep the boat on a track, so to speak. When a sailor lowers it, it keeps him from side slipping. Because the centerboard fits in a well, it can be lowered and placed in a pin, in the hole to keep it from going any farther. I sailed along on a beautiful summer day with a light, off-shore breeze. I had the wind on my port side and was on a line west, as best as I could tell for about two hours. I was barely able to see land off of my port, and up ahead I made out the sight of land on the horizon. I just sat back and enjoyed the ride, when all of the sudden the centerboard started to come up out of the well. I sat there, looked at it, and thought what in the hell is making it do that? It was my introduction to Kelly Island Shoals. The centerboard had hit bottom and was being pushed up by the shallow water of the shoal. The rudder was built for just such a problem, but it was too grounded. It had a pivot bolt that let it bend also, so I bumped across the shoals, and by some miracle, made it to Put-In-Bay. We sailed the next day and took a sixth place. There were two more races, but I can't remember how we did. I found out where Put-In-Bay was and I was introduced to the Kelly Island Shoals.

Another of my adventures occurred also while I was a student at Irving Junior High School, where we had a teacher, Miss Long, and another named Miss Lane. We were about 14 or 15 at that time, and in 8th or 9th grade, just old enough to think we had all the answers. We also started to notice that girls were different than boys. I fell in love with a girl, Olive Burkhart, who did not know that I existed, then later on, I fell head over heels for a little five feet, five inches tall gal named Esther Smith. She was a wonderful gal whom I left behind when I joined the Navy.

At that time I loafed around with Bob Miller with whom I went duck hunting. One time I took two of my buddies to a brothel in Huron, Ohio. It was the first time that I had ever been with a woman, and I was a nervous wreck during the entire trip. We went in the place, and the girl there was actually beautiful! Of course, because we were young and inexperienced, the whole thing was over in five minutes.

School was a bore to me. I had a paper route and a part-time job with Hume's Builders, standing guard over newly poured concrete, so I had a few dollars to spend. I was living with my grandmother, because my mother was in a TB sanitarium. I met a kid, named Gene Connon, who was a really nice guy about three years older than I was. He had a 1929 Ford coupe for sale for $15. I got the money together and bought it; there were no papers or anything. The car was in fair shape, and the engine ran well. I parked it behind my grandmother's house, near her kitchen. I wasn't allowed to drive it, but I could run it or just tinker with it. Well, I raced the engine so hard one day that my grandmother came out and hollered at me, saying that I was shaking the dishes off the shelves in her pantry. As kids often do, I sneaked the car out on the road, drove it up the alley behind the school, and parked it behind McFadden's garage. Boy was I something! Some of the kids wanted to go for a ride, so they jumped in. The gas pedal was round, and I had a hole in my shoe, on which the pedal was caught. All of the sudden, we were going backward too fast, and I smashed into McFadden's garage door. He raised rabbits. The impact of my car knocked over their cage, sending the bunnies running everywhere. Well, I got my car away from the garage, parked it, and went into school. I sat in class looking out of the window at 4th Street, when the kids behind me said, "Hey Bob, isn't that your car?" I looked, and sure enough, there went my car being towed by a wrecker down the street with a police car following it. About an hour later, the teacher came up to me and told me to go down to the principal's office. When I arrived, there was a police officer sitting with my mom and dad. I asked what the matter was. The cop explained to my parents what had happened. My dad had very little money in those days, and he was about to kill me. My mom, dad, and the policeman advised me that Mc Fadden wanted his garage door to be repaired and was mad as hell. I told the cop that I would pay for any damages, and he assured me that I would have to sell my car and would have to work the rest of the cost of the door off. He ordered, "No more cars!" I agreed, and they let me go. My dad told my mother that they were raising another Al Capone.

The next day I went over to McFadden and introduced myself, which was my mother's idea. I told them how sorry I was and offered them $10.00 to help to pay for the door. As it turned out, Jack McFadden, who was about 14 years old, and I struck up to be good buddies. I spent a lot of time at his house playing cards, games, and taking care of the rabbits. After some time, Mrs. McFadden told me to forget about the rest of the payment, that their insurance covered the rest. Ironically, they sold their home and moved out of town, after a guy named Potts bought it. When I came home from the war, I was living in the four-family apartment next door. One day Potts came over to the fence and asked if I wanted to buy the house. He was asking $8,500 for it, but I just did not have that kind of money. We ended up buying the place and still live there today!

After Irving Junior High, I attended Lorain High. About half way through mid-term in the tenth grade, I quit school and joined the Navy. On leave from the Navy, I went back to Irving and met with my old Manual Training teacher, Mr. Reard, a wiry old guy, who didn't mince any words. I recall one time when he said to a kid, "I bet you get out of the bath tub to take a leak." I never forgot that; why, I don't know. I still don't know what it means.

During that time of my life Don McGrady and Kenny Easton built a boathouse on Harmon's beach next to the Ohio Edison plant. Those two guys started a fishing guide service up to Middle Bass Island. They bought a home up there and had it fixed up as a Bed and Breakfast for ice fishermen. The next winter, they built ice shanties and fit out all kinds of gear for the next season. Well, for the first time in forty years, there was no ice, and they lost their shirts. So closer to home, they built this beautiful boathouse, which was forty feet long, by twenty-five feet wide. When they started building rowboats in it, we guys used to go over there to watch and to admire their wood work. They built a few more boats and then got into duck hunting. By then, Ohio Edison bought the Wickens property, on which their structure was built, and tore down their business. Kenny and Don rented a boathouse next door, owned by the Guan Family, which was an old shack with holes all over. They stored their decoys and gear in this place on the beach. They didn't know it, but some of those decoys fell out of their crates, and we kids ended up with some of those beautiful cedar decoys.

Me at 16 years old on my sailboat

CHAPTER 3 - THE DESTROYER
"NON SIBI SED PATRIAE"
NOT FOR SELF, BUT FOR COUNTRY

SOMETIMES USED NAVY MOTTO

Hitler was making news in the papers, and war was going on overseas. Guys were starting to sign up for the service, and I was sixteen years old. My mom and dad were driving across the Sandusky Bay Bridge when we heard about Pearl Harbor. My days of playing and lying around the beach were fast coming to an end. The sailboats in Harmon's started to disappear as guys left for the service. At that time, we had a bull dog named Bing, with whom I used to play down at the beach. I could throw a rock; he would go under the water and bring it back. It was my 17th birthday, and I had just signed up for the Navy. The day that I left, my dad took Bing down to the lake, which was rough. The sailboat that I had sailed for Art O'Hara had broken loose from its mooring and was damaged. My dad threw a stick in the water for Bing to retrieve—he went it after it, and never came back. That day, my dog died, my sailboat was busted up, and I was on my way to Great Lakes Training Center in Green Bay, Wisconsin.

My life had changed—no clean clothes from Mom, no hugs, no "Good night, Bobby." The world suddenly jumped up and hit me in the face.

"Hey kid, you're a man now. Wake up! Stand Guard at this post, and stay awake, or you'll get shot!"

Wow! What the hell did I get into here?

"Hey, that skivvy shirt has dirt around your neck. Run four laps around that drill field—you and the rest of the squad."

All of the sudden I was the cause of other guys made to answer for my faults. God, this is a whole new world. I soon learned the meaning of taking responsibility for my actions. The Navy training was hard to accept, but it took a kid and prepared me for a life that included killing. The only thing that I had ever killed was a blackbird with my BB gun.

My uncle gave me a trumpet, so I learned a few notes on my own, and I did know how to blow "Taps." Therefore, I joined the Drum and Bugle Corps at the base. When I wasn't on the drill field, I was in the survival pool, learning to swim under burning water, or going through gas mask training. I volunteered for a test of mustard gas and was burned with it to see how it reacted on me. Nothing ever came of it that I know. The training left me with a whole new sense of pride and respect for authority. I then had to become a man and was totally self sufficient to wash my own clothes, brush my teeth, learn how to shoot a gun, and fight hand-to-hand. The Navy made no joke about it; it was kill or be killed. Movies showed us how ships' crews survived, and what we may experience as we trained to be sailors in the U. S. Navy.

Our days were crammed with training to work as a group. When one guy made a mistake, we were all punished for it. It later paid off as we went aboard ships. Our days were so filled with training that we didn't have much time to get homesick. At night when I stood guard duty, I had lots of time to think, and it was hard not to miss my former life as free as a bird, with little or no responsibility. Now my life and the lives of my shipmates were at stake. It made me wonder if I was able to live up to that challenge.

Our first days at Great Lakes were the hardest. I did not know anyone, and I was new to this way of life. After I got to know some of the guys, I felt as though I was part of this great unit. It became more interesting, and the routine of exercise was not only building my mind but also my body. I put on weight and muscle as we trained day in and day out. The drill instructors kept us going. I remember the first thing they did when we got there was to check our teeth. Some of the guys that had to have dental work done were put in what they called Dental Company. They had to lag behind on their training and didn't get to graduate until later on.

I left Great Lakes in 1943, and was on my way to serve duty on a ship. What ship, I did not know. We boarded a train and headed east with no idea where we were going. As it turned out, we ended up on Pier 92 in New York Harbor. Word got around that the ship that I was assigned to had been sunk. The name of the ship was the *U. S. S. Mayrant, DD-402*. The ship was in the Mediterranean, near Italy at that time. We spent our time at Pier 92 wondering what and where we would end up. After a time, a Bosun asked me if was interested in becoming a Navy diver. The ocean liner, *Normandy*, was sunk at the pier next door to Pier 92, and the Navy was involved in raising her and training divers. I was kind of apprehensive, but signed up for the divers' course. After three days of training, I was told that my ship was in port over in Oran, Africa, and I could still change my mind and join the ship. I agreed, and off I went to Norfolk, Virginia, where I boarded a small Jeep aircraft carrier, named the *Mission Bay*, which was loaded with P-47 fighter planes headed for Africa. We left port and met with a large convoy. Unknown to me, at the time, my cousin, Bill Coats, whom I had grown up with, was a member of the crew on the *Mission Bay*. I crossed the ocean with him and never knew he was there.

The crossing was uneventful, and we got off in Casablanca, amid a harbor covered with sunken ships. One was the French battle wagon, the *Jean Bart*. After leaving the *Mission Bay*, we were loaded into box cars and started our train ride to Oran. The train had about 25 to 30 cars, all loaded with Army units going up to North Africa. Our car carried about 15 to 20 Navy guys going to catch their ships on the north shore of Africa.

During that two-day trip, I was really impressed with the Navy, because the Army guys were eating K-Rations, and we had Dole pineapple juice, spam, and fresh baked bread. Don't ask me how the Navy did it, but it did! It was comical to watch when the train stopped once in a while to take on water or wood, all the guys ran to the side of the tracks to do their thing. When the train blew its whistle, which meant, "Get going! If you're not on the train, you're going to have to walk!" Guys ran with their pants half down in order to make the boxcar before it left them. Yet, across the northern part of Africa, I saw some beautiful mountains while on that train.

After we got to Oran, we went to Mers-El-Kebir, through a long, long tunnel to the dock area on the Mediterranean. My ship, the *DD-402*, was at the dock. I came aboard and was introduced to the crew and the executive officer, Lieutenant Franklin D. Roosevelt, Jr. The ship had been hit by a 500 pound bomb off of Palermo, Sicily. By luck, she was heading home for repairs. The battleship, *U. S. S. Iowa*, was also in port there, and President Roosevelt was meeting with Prime Minister Churchill on it. The president had a chance to see his son, Frank, while I had the opportunity to be near some very important people.

After a day or so, we left Oran with a small convoy and sailed up to the Rock of Gibraltar. We docked there and soon found out that the place was loaded with monkeys or baboons. They just wandered around like they owned the place! After taking on fuel and supplies, we left Gibraltar and joined a convoy headed for the states. Our one engine was out of commission, so we were limited in speed and maneuverability, but we still served as an effective escort. We chased contacts with subs, and on two or three occasions, we were worried about the patch that was welded over the damaged hole from the bomb. The jarring from the depth charges weakened it, yet we continued on our way, doing our job as an escort to protect the merchant ships.

On the third day out of Gibraltar, we encountered a three-day hurricane. Waves became fifty to seventy-five feet high, and our ship was beginning to break apart at the bow, which rolled one way, while the stern rolled the other. We heard the metal creak and grind. Merchant ships, a hundred yards away, disappeared behind the waves. Our destroyer looked like we had to shift gears to make it up the next wave. We survived and made the crossing fairly unscathed and ended up in the dry dock in Charleston, South Carolina.

In early 1944, after we came out of the shipyard in Charleston, we were sent to submarine patrol in the North Atlantic. It was miserable duty in freezing weather and rough seas. Once in a while, we pulled into Casco Bay, Maine, to get more depth charges. On one occasion, I was taking the skipper into the dock from our anchorage out in the bay. I was in charge of whale boat duty. When we pulled into a small dock at the Officer's Club there, we left the Captain off the boat. As I was about to leave, I saw two large milk cans on the dock. I looked around to see if anyone was there, then told my deck hand to grab them and to bring them aboard the whale boat. Fresh milk was not something we saw every day! We smuggled the cans aboard the ship, took them up in the forepeak, and hid them, setting them way up on a shelf. We talked a cook into some eggs and sugar, and then made eggnog. We ran a siphon hose down and had the delicious drink for the crew. Well lo and behold, a massive investigation was started over the missing milk cans. It seems as though they were the personal property of the admiral. Needless to say, no one on our destroyer knew anything about that!

Fifty years later, I sent a letter to the *Tin Can Newspaper*, a destroyer paper for vets, which went like this: "The case of the missing milk cans, Admiral, if you're still alive, I am sorry. I admit that I took your milk cans up to Casco Bay. My conscience has bothered me for over 50 years. DAMN, IT WAS GOOD!"

After that, we were around Nova Scotia when we received a radio message, informing us that a tanker had been torpedoed eighty miles off of Boston. We got underway immediately, and ran full speed all the way down to Boston. The weather was rough, and when we sighted the tanker, she was sinking stern first. The crew had abandoned ship. As we approached the tanker, our skipper decided to take the tanker in tow and to bring it into Boston. The ocean was also very rough, and the stern of the tanker was awash. As waves broke, the stern went under, came up, and dumped the water off. We put the whale boat in the water, and then five of us went over and boarded the tanker. We had to be careful not to be sucked on deck when the stern went under. We jumped aboard the tanker, while our destroyer came alongside and passed us a heaving line. We played out an 8-inch manila tow line. There was no power on the ship, and the line was heavy. The ship, *U. S. S. Atlantic States*, had been hit by an acoustic torpedo that ran up her wake and hit her stern. The rudder was jammed over to port, and as we tried to tow her, she wanted to go that way, making a circle.

After about an hour, we made only about a half a mile, and the tow line broke. We spliced a new eye in the line and played out some more tow line from the hold. We towed the ship for about ten hours and made about ten miles, when the line broke again. We got more line out, and no more started a tow, when the destroyer dropped the tow line and left us. It had picked up a contact on sonar. We were stuck with hauling in all that wet line by hand. It was so heavy that we gave up and just dropped it back and got another line. The contact turned out to be a school of red snapper. Many times we covered the ocean with dead fish from dropping charges on false alarm fish schools. Anyway, we could not take any chances—sub or fish—we just dropped the depth charges to find out.

The sun came out, and it was a nice day. We found some food lockers and set up a table on deck. We ate until we couldn't breathe. There was milk, cake and all kinds of stuff that we had not seen for quite a while. After spending a night on the sinking tanker, we were met by a sea-going tug. We passed a tow line to it and soon were on our way to Boston. It was an eerie feeling being on a ship with no crew. Bulkhead doors swung back and forth. When we looked down into the engine room, water was splashing back and forth. Otherwise, the ship was dead silent. As we passed the entrance to the port of Boston, I reflected on my experience and the date. What a way to spend my birthday!

We made about two more crossings to Africa and to Italy. In the last crossing, we joined up with a convoy off of Norfolk, Virginia. Our Destroyer squadron of the *U. S. S. Tripe, Wainright, Stack* and two others set up a screen, and we were underway, headed for Naples, Italy. The convoy had to have about thirty-five ships. We soon found out that it was a six-knot convoy. We set up our pattern of zigzag, and day after day, it was the same old slow motion. Occasionally, we received a contact on the sonar and ran over to check it out. Sometimes we ended up dropping depth charges, while at other times, we found schools of fish. It got to the point that only torpedo men manned the K-guns and depth charge racks. We didn't even sound "general quarters." The weather turned bad, and at slow speed, we labored—bad rock and roll—not fun at all.

During that time, they sounded chow call on the P.A., so I went down to the galley and grabbed a tray to get in line. When I got to the servers, they had spaghetti and meatballs. I took my tray and sat down at the table. Suddenly the ship took a hard roll, and my spaghetti slithered out of my tray, ran down the table and off onto the deck. I said to myself," Oh, the hell with it. I'm not too hungry anyway." I got up and walked out of the passageway and on to the open deck. A wave broke over the bow and poured right down my neck. I ran back to the after-deckhouse, dropped down the stairs, and opened my locker to get a candy bar. They were all gone. Later on they opened the small locker when they kept the candy and stuff on deck, so I grabbed my pea coat and stuffed a $20 bill in my pocket. I got up on deck where it was blowing a gale. I got to the "Pogie Bait") [Navy-speak for candy] shop and felt a piece of paper in my pocket. Without thinking, I grabbed it and tossed it up in the air. I finally realized that the wind blew away my twenty bucks out to the middle of the Atlantic. I often wondered where that twenty dollar bill had ended up—probably on the bottom of the Atlantic Ocean.

We passed the Azores and headed for the Rock of Gibraltar. There, we found out that German Planes and subs had been very active of late, so we were told to make smoke to cover our convoy. We welcomed that, as it gave us an opportunity to come up to speed and run up and down the convoy. When we arrived in Naples, Italy, we heard two American pilots hollering over the radio. They were P-47 pilots in a dogfight with a bunch of German fighter planes. From what we heard, one of our P-47 pilots was shot down, and we were about to go see if we were able to help. The report came from around the Isle of Capri, so we left the convoy to look for the downed pilot, with no results.

Afterwards, we entered the harbor at Naples and tied up. The town was built on the side of a mountain, or a large hill. In it were beautiful, white buildings. We were given liberty and soon went ashore, looking the place over. Shortly a young kid came running up to us and hollered, "Hey Joe! Want an American piece of ass?" We could not believe our ears! We asked him what he had just said, and he repeated it. My buddy told him that he would take him up on his offer, so the kid hollered back, "Go f—your—self." My other buddy and I laughed until our sides hurt.

Later on we climbed about a thousand stairs and came across a line of sailors and other guys. We walked up and asked what was going on. One of the men looked at us as though we had come from Mars, and said, "Get in line. It's a whorehouse!" I counted, and there were sixteen guys in line. I looked over to my buddy and asked if he wanted us to be 17 and 18. He said, "Hell, no," so we left and bumped into two really nice-looking Italian gals. They were way ahead of us, and although they were nice about it, they let us know that they did not plan on going to bed with us. They laughed and joked with us, but our sign language didn't help the situation either. I chanced upon a small gift shop, and as we looked through the place, I came across an ornament that caught my eye. It was a symbol of "Pompa," which was a man's penis with wings. I bought one, and after the war, I hung it on my convertible. Girls looked at it, snickered, but never said a thing.

The next day we got underway and headed for the straits of Gibraltar. We noticed a huge gathering of warships and support ships. The sea was covered with ships of all sizes, because the invasion of southern France was about to begin. We ran at 25 knots and had all of our main batteries manned and ready. We stood gun watches all of the time in that area. We passed Gibraltar and headed out to sea. I stood gun watch on #2. 5-inch 38 gun and it was 2:00 a.m., or 200 hours. I walked around the gun and spotted a large bird sitting there asleep. I sneaked up and grabbed him. Just as fast, he latched on to my arm. I thought, "Damn! This bird has got some beak!" He drew blood! I had a hold of an albatross, and he was mad. Then the thought came to me that there were a bunch of guys down below who were asleep. I thought, "I will take this great, big bird down and dump him in my buddy's bunk." I threw him in the bunk, and all hell broke loose. Guys were screaming and hollering. The whole ship woke up. The deck officer came down to the compartment and wanted to know how that bird got in there. No one knew anything about it. He came up to the gun mount and asked us if we saw anything. We acted dumb, and after they left, we busted a gut laughing.

The next night we were standing gun mount watch, and we heard general quarters go off. The ship picked up speed, and we ran after a ship contact that did not answer our challenge. We were up to speed, running 30 knots with all guns trained out on the target. Suddenly our searchlight came on, and there was a little coastal steamer. The ship's captain came out of the pilothouse, half asleep, looking at a destroyer going 30 knots, running past him with all guns aimed at him. I often wondered how he felt. Once the searchlight showed his colors, he was free to carry on. We went by so fast that I don't know if he had seen us or not, but if he did, he won't forget for a long time, because we passed within thirty feet of his vessel.

At Sandy Point the next morning, we unloaded all of our ammunition. We then went into Brooklyn Navy Yard and received a 24-hour pass. I decided to take a chance and grab a train home. My dad had joined the Army and was up in Alaska. My mother was working in the shipyard, so I figured that I could see her for a few hours anyway. I took a cab to Penn Station and went to buy a ticket home. I was short $15, so I grabbed a sailor passing by and asked to borrow the money, which he gave me, and I jumped on the train. I got to Cleveland, and the Shore Patrol nabbed me. I was outside of the hundred-mile limit on a 24-hour pass. They took me in, and when the Officer of the Day (O.D.) heard my story, he made them take me back and get me on a bus to Lorain. My mother didn't know that I was coming, and she was happy to see me, but disappointed to hear that I had to run back. I had a three-hour visit before I returned to New York. I got back to ship, only to learn that we had another 24-hour pass. My buddy and I left the ship and went up to Times Square. We had a bet with two other guys that we could get a shot and a beer in every bar between Times Square and Rockefeller Center, and then go ice skating at the Rockefeller Center Ice Rink. Well I don't think we missed too many bars, but by the time we got to Rockefeller Center and went skating, we entertained a crowd before the Shore Patrol led us away.

The next day we got underway, loaded our ammo, and headed up to Boston to load up more depth charges. We docked and were informed that we had liberty for 24 hours. We had heard about Riviera Beach Amusement Park near Boston, so we headed up that way. We found the place which had all kinds of rides, and it looked to be a lot of fun. As we walked down to the roller coaster, we noticed a gal, with a big pair of boobs, about to get on the ride. I bet my buddy that I could have those boobs out before the end of the ride. He took the wager. I ran up and jumped in the car with her. I explained the bet to her; she was a great sport. She went along with it, and by the time we got back to the start, I had one boob out. The crowd waiting at the ride, roared. She came over to meet my buddy. Afterwards, we took her out and bought her a dinner. She was a great gal and told us that she was joining the Army Air Force the next day. We left her and went back to the ship.

The rumor mill was going full blast—we are going to France;—we are going to South America;—we are going to Alaska. As it turned out, we started to operate out of Boston Harbor. We soon learned "the lay of the land," so to speak, and found gals in Skull Square, in Lynn, Mass and Salem. One gal in Salem caught my eye. She was a five feet, seven inches tall, Irish gal who lived on Gallows Hill in Salem. Her name was O'Connell. I fell in love with her, and we were married. She was a lot of fun, and her parents were great people. I wasn't married for just over two weeks, when we were ordered to ship out. It was hard to leave her, as anyone in love knows. As we got underway, we found out that we were heading for the West Coast. We ran south with the cruiser, *Astoria*, as she began her sea trials. We left her off at South America and entered the Panama Canal. We heard that the war was over in Europe, that Germany surrendered. We passed through the locks and headed up the Mexican coast. We stopped over at San Diego. Erroll Flynn, the movie star's yacht was just across the bay from us. I hated the place right away. It was hot all day, then rained, and was cold at night. As we came up the Mexican coast, the weather was beautiful, and we saw a lot of big turtles swimming out there. For some reason, I could not wait to leave the place.

After a short stay, we were underway to Pearl Harbor, where we took on fuel and supplies; then we headed for Saipan with a small convoy. There was a small island just south of Saipan called Rota. It had a small consignment of Japs on the island and was bypassed by our forces as not worth the trouble to fight over. We learned that fact from some Air Force pilots whom we met on Saipan. When these pilots came back from a bomb run, they strafed the outhouses that were on cliffs that overhung the ocean, so the Japs never even got a chance to take a crap in peace.

On ship, we had a guy named Ristanko, from Cleveland, who was about six feet, three or four inches tall and weighed about 300 pounds. When we went on shore leave, we always took him along, so that if there was a fight, we had him to take care of us.

Well we pulled into the dock at Saipan in the Pacific and laid along side another destroyer that had been hit by Jap planes. There were other destroyers docked there as well. The crew on the damaged destroyer asked if we wanted to join in their boxing match. We agreed. They told us to get a few guys who wanted to box, and we could wager some money. We immediately thought of Ristanko! God, we had it made with him; we couldn't lose! The next day they set up a makeshift ring on the stern of the other destroyer, and we had Ristanko all set to go. This guy looked like he could kill a tiger with his bare hands. He told us that he drank raw chicken blood when he could get it.

Well, we got over to the ring and Ristanko stepped into it. Here came a little guy who was about five feet, six inches tall and skinny as hell! He stepped into the ring. Our crew started looking at each other; we began counting our winnings, because we had it made! The bell rang and each guy got up to run to the center of the ring. They started to jab and size up each other. All of the sudden, the little guy wound up and hit Ristanko square on the jaw. If you ever saw a giant redwood tree fall—that was Ristanko. He went down like a ton of bricks. The crew and I looked at each other and turned white. My God! He had a glass jaw. We could have gotten killed on liberty with him! We used to feel safe in the bars with Ristanko along. That feeling ended with the count of 10.

We left Saipan and ran up to Iwo Jima with a load of Marines aboard. The island had been secured by that time, and the Marines were just being sent up for clean-up duty. We anchored off of the island and dropped off the Marines. We were then ordered to proceed to Chichi Jima. We entered a large bay in the island and picked up an Australian lookout observer who had been on the island for four months. We returned him to Saipan and picked up a convoy for Okinawa. We pulled into Okinawa at Buckner Bay, and then we got underway back to Iwo Jima, but we had to fuel up at sea during our return.

After the island had been secured, we anchored just off the beach near Iwo Jima. We were tired and needed some rest and relaxation. I went to the stern of the ship, just to take it easy. The weather was hot and sunny which made the deck warm. I just sat down, leaned on the rail, and closed my eyes. I kind of fell asleep. I awakened, just as the cook came back to dump some garbage over the stern. The water was so clear that you could see a hundred feet down or more. As I sat there, I noticed a small fish come up and grab a piece of potato skin and then swim away. There came another, then another, and pretty soon, there was a large blue streak flying by which nailed that small 12—to 15-inch bait fish that had grabbed the potato skin. Well my mind started to wonder how in the hell I could get one of those big fish. I went forward and got a whole coil of 21—thread (that's like clothesline). I rigged a hook and leader from a life raft, and then we rigged a small net. With the help of the cook and some garbage, we caught some small bait fish. At this time, the crew started to gather around and watched us. When I put the large coil of line down and hooked up the leader, they laughed. But when I tied the end of the line to a stanchion on the stern, they laughed their asses off. Well I baited the hook and cast the coil of line overboard. It sank in easy view to about fifty feet down. A monster blue streak grabbed it and took that line sizzling off of that deck. Within a few seconds, it came to an end, went "pow!" and broke. It didn't take long before fifty guys were back on the stern with hand lines catching beautiful blue tuna. We landed 14 of them that day on hand lines, with the captain and crew all involved. We had been eating Australian mutton for over a month, and these tuna saved our lives. They were "deeeluscious!" If anyone wants to fish for tuna, that's the place to do it. Each was 40 to 60 pounds, and there were loads of them.

At one point, we dropped anchor in a bay near the Ulithy Atoll, at a little island named Mog Mog, which was nothing more than a sandbar in the middle of the Pacific Ocean. Well they gave each of us a few cans of beer and ran us over to this little island and told us to have fun. It had to be 110 degrees in the shade. There was not a cloud in the sky, and here we sat drinking beer, looking at the ocean. I drank one beer and gave the rest to my buddy, Warren Roberts, from Sandusky, Ohio. I don't think there was a tree on that island, so I just took a walk and went exploring. I waded along the shoreline, barefoot, and enjoyed the day, just relaxing.

As I sit here writing this book, I believe this island was later a part of the atom bomb testing. After the war ended, our ship, the *U.S.S. Mayrant, DD-402*, met her end as part of those atomic bomb tests.

But back on that day in 1944, we had no idea what the future would bring. Soon the whale boat came and got us, and we returned to the ship. That was our "R and R" for the year! Looking back at those times, I believe that the Navy did a great job of trying to make life bearable. We had a bunk to sleep in and three meals a day. The foot soldiers, God bless them, had the dirty job of digging the Japs out of holes in the ground on these islands. A friend of mine, in later life, an ex-Marine talked about the war and the islands, and how the Navy had bombarded the islands before the invasions. He told me, "You know something? You guys missed a lot of them bastards!" It is funny now, but not then. As I look back on my service aboard the ship, I recall how at night one time, as we were passing close to some of the islands in the Pacific, if I just jumped overboard and swam on the beach, I could spend the rest of the war, just laying on the sand, eating coconuts, and living a life of east under a palm tree. Then I woke up from my dream and realized that if I had swum over there to an island, I may have gotten greeted with a Japanese bayonet. Thus, I said to myself, this life on this ship was pretty good at that! I loved the ocean and the beauty of the sea and sky out in the Pacific. The different colors of the water and its clarity were just beautiful!

When we operated with a carrier or a cruiser, and a plane ditched or a float plane had to be destroyed by gun fire, I used to think, boy, if I had a tug and salvaged that plane! You can see that I was a dreamer then also. The cost of the war was beyond belief, not only in lives lost, but also with the staggering loss of ships, aircraft, and equipment. But, I guess that is the price we had to pay in this world of ours. Our next stop was in the Mariana Islands and Saipan, I think.

As the war went on, we wondered what it would take to end this conflict. We were now in the western Pacific on what was called picket duty. Our job was to report any aircraft incoming toward Okinawa. We were very fortunate that we were not attacked, and we served out that duty with no incidents.

When we returned to Okinawa and anchored just before dark, a Jap plane flew over our stern and dropped an aerial torpedo that hit the battleship, *Pennsylvania,* in the stern. As we left port in the morning, they were pumping her out because her stern was pretty much down in the water. As we passed, we all came to attention and saluted an old warrior. We left there and headed back to Iwo Jima. Our orders were to pick up a small convoy to take it to Saipan. When we got to Iwo, we received the news that Hiroshima had been destroyed with one bomb. My God! What kind of bomb was that? The next city to be razed by the atomic bomb was Nagasaki, and the Japanese surrendered as a result.. We then looked forward to going home.

When the atomic bomb was dropped, and the war with Japan ended in the Pacific, we were ordered to take the ship to Marcus Island and to accept the surrender of all enemy forces on the island. We ran down to Marcus Island, and as we pulled in to anchor, the water was so clear that I saw the bottom of the ocean as though it was ten feet deep. The captain did not believe the sonar and ordered us to throw a lead line. We cast a lead line out, and there was no bottom at 150 feet. We anchored and were informed that the Japanese were to disarm all ordnance and to place a large white cross on their airfield to signal their surrender. A commodore was sent over to the island to accept the surrender. He arrived on another destroyer and came aboard our ship. After some discussions, the captain and the commodore got in my whale boat for a trip over to the island to accept the Japs' surrender. As I left the ship with them, I got half way to the beach, and all hell broke loose. The island erupted in explosions! Stuff was flying everywhere. Needless to say, I was ordered to turn around and to head back to the ship. After our return to the ship, we found out that the Japs had started to move ammunition in accordance with the surrender plans and a truck had turned over and exploded. Again, we started in to take the surrender. After the commodore, captain, and a Japanese interpreter left the boat to raise the American flag, my boat hook and I sat in the whale boat. Soon we became bored and left the whale boat. We took a walk over to another part of the island. We had a Thompson submachine gun with us, so we felt safe. Soon after that, we saw the surrender party coming back to the whale boat. The only way we could get back to the boat without them seeing us was to jump over a hill and a trench and run down to the beach, which is what we did. We beat them to the boat, took the party back to the ship, and felt that we were safe. The next day the entire crew was offered to go ashore to take pictures. We, however, were on report and confined to the ship because we had been seen, from the ship, running down to the beach. As we stood looking at the beach the next day, we noticed a few Japs on the beach doing something. I walked up to the Officer of the Deck and asked what the hell they were doing over there. He looked at me and said, "They are digging up land mines that you two assholes ran over yesterday." Suddenly, my legs felt weak. Our guardian angel was at work that day!

When we got to Tinnian Island, near Saipan, some pilots got a chance to be at the Japanese surrender on the battleship, *Missouri.* They had some copies of the event, and talked one pilot from Ohio into giving me a set. At about that time, our skipper, Captain Otto Schirni, was relieved and sent to direct an anti-submarine school. He later became an admiral.

My story about the war would not be complete unless I mentioned a kid I grew up with—Jack Mitenbuler. We joined the service together, only Jack went into the Air Force. In 1944, I was aboard the destroyer off of Iwo Jima, and I saw a story in the *Stars and Strips* which told of Jack, a P-51 mustang pilot with the 8th Air Force, shot down over France by a German ace. Jack's wingman then shot the German plane down before both pilots bailed out and survived. The German was taken to an internment camp. Later, Jack met the guy who shot him down. They saluted each other, and became friends and often wrote to each other.

Our "mustering out" orders, as they called them, were set up on the amount of time a sailor had in the Navy. The older guys had first chance. Some stayed on and became high ranking officers in the peacetime Navy. My time up was on June 12, 1947. I left the ship at San Diego with my sea bag packed with all kinds of foul weather gear and souvenirs. I had an extra bag with stuff that I had collected, like a Japanese rifle, a German hand gun. I even had a machine gun that I picked up in Italy and hid in the forward locker. As I was about to leave the ship, it was announced over the loud speaker that there was to be an inspection of our bags as we left. I set my bag of goodies in a corner and left with only my main bag. They never did inspect our bags. I often wondered who got the goodies that I left on the ship.

The *U. S. S. Mayrant* at Anchor

Me on the bridge of the *Mayrant* on Lookout Duty

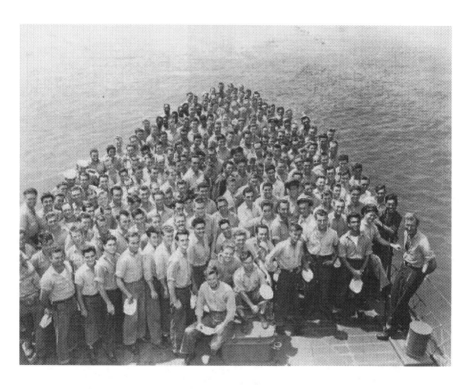

Entire *Mayrant* Crew on Ship's Bow—I'm in the Middle in Dark Jersey

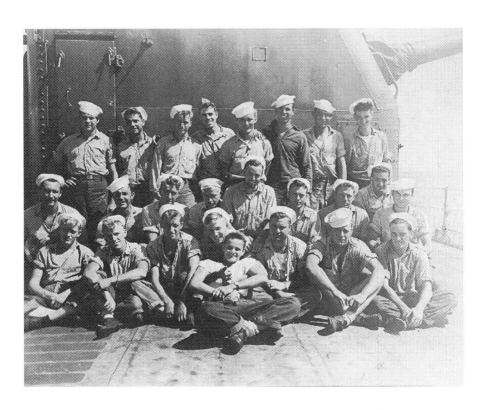

Deck Force Crew—I'm Third from Right, Top Row

U.S.S. Mayrant Refueling at Sea from Tanker

U.S.S. Mayrant at Anchor near Iwo Jima Island

Tinnian Island Air Force B-29 Base
Place from which the *Enola Gay* Took Off

Japanese Officers Surrender Party at Marcus Island

**Actual Pictures of Surrender of Japanese to
MacArthur—World War II**

U. S. S. MAYRANT
(DD 402)

FLEET POST OFFICE
NEW YORK, N. Y.

11 April 1945

From: The Commanding Officer.
To   :   J.:YCOX, Robert Allen, 265 34 44, Cox, USNR.

Subject: Meritorious Duty - Performance of.

1.   You are hereby commended for displaying outstanding
seamanship and devotion to duty in assisting with the towing and
salvage of a torpedoed merchant tanker in rough seas.

C.T.P'S.T..I   O. A. SCHIRNI.

Commendation from Captain Schirni

Robert A. JAYCOX

To you who answered the call of your country and served in its Armed Forces to bring about the total defeat of the enemy, I extend the heartfelt thanks of a grateful Nation. As one of the Nation's finest, you undertook the most severe task one can be called upon to perform. Because you demonstrated the fortitude, resourcefulness and calm judgment necessary to carry out that task, we now look to you for leadership and example in further exalting our country in peace.

Harry Truman

THE WHITE HOUSE

Letter of Gratitude from President Truman

CHAPTER 4
ROWBOATS, POWER BOATS AND PLANES

A LAKE CARRIES YOU INTO RECESSES
OF FEELING OTHERWISE IMPENETRABLE

WILLIAM WORDSWORTH

I left the ship and boarded a train for Ohio. The ride home was long and dirty. When we arrived in Cleveland, I took a bus home. We were living on the East Side again, at Nebraska Avenue. My parents purchased a home there during the war. As I got off the bus at Nebraska Avenue, with my sea bag and the one Jap rifle they let me take, my little sister, Lynne, came running down the road to meet me. I hardly had a chance to know her after being away all of those years, but it was great to be home again and to see my sis. Our home was the second to the last on the street, on the west side. My mom and dad were there to greet me. It was a great time to be home and safe. My wife, Evelyn, whom I married in Boston, was to arrive the next day; I was in heaven! About a week went by and everything was going fine, when my mother informed me that she and my dad heard a strange conversation on the phone between a guy from out in California and my wife. They were saying some really strange stuff, according to my parents. When I came home that day after looking for a job, I confronted her about the phone calls. To make a long story short, she had married three guys and was living on our service allotments. I helped her to pack her bags and put her on a bus for home. Two months later, I received news that she was in prison in Framingham, Massachusetts. That was the last I ever heard from her. I got a divorce and just about went crazy. The love that I had held all of the time that I was in the Pacific was destroyed!

My first introduction to the powerboat field began when I had my first rowboat, which I resurrected from down at the beach. The boat had been abandoned, and was a total wreck. I took it home to rebuild it. It was not pretty, but it floated. I bought an old Evinrude engine from a kid for $10. It had a knob on top of the flywheel, and it was started by spinning the knob around. After I got it running, it was so out of balance that it just about shook the boat apart. It was all I had, and it got me out to the lighthouse to fish. Later on, I built a rowboat in the cellar of my mom's house on Nebraska. I had just returned from the Navy, and I wanted to be back out on the lake. I had never built a boat, but as kids, we used to watch the boat builders back in those days.

I had no plans, but I had a good idea of what I wanted. I bought some wood, screws, and started out. I made a bow post first, and slowly, but surely, got my first boat built. I used it first to get out to the breakwater to hunt ducks, then later on to pull gill nets. I had to make some adjustments to the boat because there was not enough freeboard, so I just built it up by adding another board to the rail. We used to go out in some nasty weather with that old boat. We used to fish three gill nets at about 300 feet.

One day, in the spring; it was March and cold out. The ice had just opened up in the lake and we got out to set the nets off of Lakeview Park. The wind was blowing out of the northwest, and the water was rough. Waves were rolling into the beach, and there was white water all over the lake. I got a hold of my old friend, Joe Berry, and asked if he wanted to help me pull nets. It was done all by hand. He agreed, and we both went down to Harmon's beach, where I kept the boat docked. Now remember this, it is a little 16 foot homemade rowboat with a 2.5 horsepower Elgin-Sears engine. When we got underway, it was nice inside the breakwater, but I had to go through the gap in the wall to get out to the open lake. The waves were rolling in through the gap. I had to wait for just the right moment to head out through the gap to avoid a breaking wave. Suddenly I had my chance! I gunned the engine wide open, and we shot through the gap. Just then a large wave broke and we went up in the air and came down hard. The center seat broke in half, and Joe ended up on the bottom of the boat. The seat plank had been the main beam to hold the sides in place, so then the chines were breaking apart. The sides of the boat were waving at us. Joe hollered for us to go back. I told him, "Hell, we are out here now; let's just pull the nets, then go in." Joe bailed water, while I sped the boat down to Lakeview about a half a mile away. We got to the nets and started to pull them. They were full of walleyes; so many, in fact, that the little boat was about to swamp. We got the nets and fish aboard and headed back. We were running with the sea while each wave tried to broach us. We got to the gap in the wall, and again, I waited for the right time to make my move to enter the gap. A big wave ran by us, and I headed for the opening. Another wave caught us, and we surf-boarded through the inlet and beached right onto the sandbar. The boat was full of water, nets, and fish, and we were soaked and frozen. We got the boat onto the beach and unloaded. We took the fish up to the fish house and sold them. The sale of those fish gave us money to go to the sport show, which Virginia and I hardly ever missed. Back then, there were such great acts which used to show up there.

It was at a sport show that I decided to get into racing boats. I got started with a Wagemaker boat built in Michigan. I may have spelled that wrong, but anyway, it had a molded hull about 16 feet long, I put a 10 horsepower Mercury engine on it and bought a quicksilver lower unit for it. That boat really moved! I won lots of races with that until I was caught and racing authorities banned the use of the lower unit. Next, I got a Switzer Craft that had such a beautifully built hull which was to be used strictly for racing. I won many times with that boat, and then I got into hydroplane racing. My first hydroplane was named *Ding Dong* and the next one was *Satan's Waitin.* It was luck that I did not kill myself in those things. They were fast and easy to flip. I finally decided to give up racing and try flying. I was making up for all the years that I lost in the Navy, and the adventure-seeking boy was still inside of me.

I had a hard time adjusting to life. At that point, I took up flying and learned to fly with the help of the G. I. Bill. My instructor was Joe Puma, a fighter pilot from World War II. He and three other guys had started a flying school, and I loved it! Joe was a fantastic pilot, and as I trained with him, he often said, "Let's see if we can strafe that train," and off he went, flipping that little Aronca airplane over on its back and down we dove. I, many times, wondered what that train engineer thought as we skimmed past his engine and shot up into the sky. My instructor did a great job of teaching me to fly. I frequently bet with other pilots about how good of a pilot I was. We would go up and be flying along, and all of a sudden Joe would say, "You just lost your engine! Let's see you land!" We often practiced over the country area where fields were open lots.

On one field, the flight instructors had made a big circle with paint, and we used to see who could come closest to the center, after we cut power and glided from about 500 feet high. I got damn good at it, while Joe won some money betting on me. A young guy who had trained with me was killed when he tried to go from the back seat to the front seat. His head hit the trim tab on the overhead of the plane, and he dove into the ground.

I made my cross-country flights solo, passed my training, and got my pilot's license. Just before I did though, I had met and married my wife, Virginia. She is a great gal with all of the qualities any man would want: beautiful, intelligent, and faithful. I had her meet me in a vacant field out near Vermilion. I landed and took her up for a ride. I got her up in the plane and did a few rolls and loops. Suddenly, she threw up in the back seat. I took her back, landed in the field, and flew the plane back to the airport. I landed, and Joe, my instructor, came over to the plane and looked in. As I unbuckled my seatbelt, he said, "What in the hell did you do in the back?" He had seen all of the vomit.

I told him that I was practicing spins and got sick. I got away with it, but I don't know if Joe ever bought that story. After I got my license, I took my dad up. He sat in the back seat. As I made a few maneuvers, I looked in the mirror and noticed that he was hanging on to the tubing, and was white as snow. I, then, told him to watch, that I was going to show him how I made an emergency landing. I cut power and went down between a farmhouse and a silo into a cornfield. Just before we hit the corn, I pulled up and put the plane into a steep climb. He was hanging on and screamed, "Take me down, you crazy bastard!" I flew back to the airport, where my dad got out of the plane and did not even say goodbye. He just left!

I, of course, had to go through that time in my life where I felt very adventurous. I bought a motorcycle and was trying to catch up with my life. I missed out on my teen years and needed to have some fun. I still had the urge for sailing, so I signed up to ship out on a lake freighter. I sailed on the U. S. Steel ore boat, *Horace J. Johnson*. I was, what they called, a watchman. My job was to operate the winches and to direct the deck force. I was bunking in with a guy, who was the captain's pet. This guy thought that he owned the ship, and I was the last kid on the block. I frequently had the crew in the room to listen to the radio that I had brought along. This "captain's pet" didn't like it, so he broke off the aerial from the radio. I confronted him about it, and we got into a fight. I hit him once, and he went down. When he got up, he ran to the captain. At the next port I got off and left the ship in Huron, Ohio. I really liked that job! The food was outstanding! I had started to study to get my mate's papers, but that would have to wait.

Back at home, I bought a "new to me," used car, a 1939 Ford Coupe. I was free as a bird and looking for some company, so I stopped at the Lorain Coliseum, a roller rink. I no more than walked in the door, when I spotted this gal spinning around the rink. My cousin happened to be there, so I asked her to introduce me to this great-looking brunette. She agreed and soon had her to come over the meet me. Being a smart ass, I asked her if she had ever been told that she looked like a movie star. She told me no, so I said, "Well don't feel badly, maybe someone will, some day." I later dated her and ended up marrying her.

I got into boats and built a rowboat and started to fish. My wife and I were then living in a four-family apartment on West Erie. We had our first baby on the way. My son was born, and we were the proud parents of an 8 pound baby boy, Bobby, Jr. Times were tough then. I was working at a gas station at Oberlin and West Erie Avenues. The next boat I purchased was a hydroplane, which I raced. I won quite a few races and life was going great.

In October of 1955, the weather was great for hunting ducks. It had turned cold because of the arctic front from Canada that had moved through. I got up at 6:00 a.m. to call my good friend, Joe Berry. I asked him if he was ready, because I had called him the night before. I told him to meet me at Harmon's Beach, right in back of Joe's house. I left, and as I drove down to the beach, it started to snow half-rain and half-snow. It was miserable, yet a great day for our trip out to the wall. I had the decoys all painted up and ready. We had 2 dozen black duck decoys from Herders, and a dozen blue bills. Our boat was a 14 feet long wooden boat that I had built when I came home the Navy. It was powered by a 2.5 horsepower engine from Sears.

The waves came over the breakwater as we put the boat in the water. We ran out to the duck blind that we built and set out our decoys. We pulled the boat up on the ramp that we built and opened the drain plug. We learned that trick the hard way when once before, the boat filled up with water from the waves coming over the wall. Three waves got us good before we got into the duck blind. Ice cold water gushing down my neck at 6:30 in the morning did not feel too good. We took our guns into the blind. I had mine in a case to keep it dry because it was a beautiful Remington auto, special edition—no plugs in those days!

We had a little oil stove in the shanty, so we fired it up. Soon, it was warm to us, and we smashed a few of the large spiders that had made their home in our duck blind. We settled in to hunt. The sky was starting to lighten up in the east, and the wind was from the northwest at about 25 to 30 miles per hour. I forgot to mention that my good friend, Bob Miller was with us. He had called to ask to come along. The three of us were in the shanty, and as we talked, a bunch of blue bills—about 30 of them—had landed in the decoys. We didn't even have shells in our guns yet. Now we had a real set of decoys. We loaded up our guns and dropped the front of the blind. Joe had a double-barrel shotgun, and he was looking for his shells. I hollered at Miller to take them. We shot and dropped about 6 or 7 bills. We dumped the boat in the water, rowed out, and picked up the birds. When we got back to the blind, Joe had just finished loading his gun. We told Joe that the next bird was his. A nice big pair of blacks dropped into the decoys. We asked Joe if he was ready, and he shook his head yes, so we dropped the blind door. Joe set up to shoot. He fired the gun, but there was no noise, just a big puff, while the BBs rolled out of the barrel and dropped into the water. We laughed until our sides hurt. You see, Joe didn't believe in fresh ammunition. He used shells that were made in World War I! At any rate, the day was a duck hunter's dream: beautiful early morning sky. The birds were in flight. The waves were crashing over the wall, and it was a wonderful day to be alive.

I eventually got a job at Ohio Edison, the local power house and started at 70 cents an hour. The work was interesting, and I had a great teacher, a man named Don Rounds. Don was in his 50s, I think, and he was a Stationary Engineer. We had large generators in the plant, powered by huge steam turbines. When I first started there, the place was called OPS; that's Ohio

Public Service Company. At that time, the superintendent was Mr. McCormick, who was a strict, but fair man who liked to hire ex-servicemen. I started as an oiler, a kind of apprentice. As time went by, I had worked my way up to "B-man," then later as an engineer, after I had gotten my engineer's license. I spent 25 years in the plant was about to receive my 25-year pin and watch.

During the later years there, I had been working part-time as a commercial fisherman, and made more money part-time than I did at my full-time job, so I quit my job and went fishing after 25 years at the plant.

Picture of Great Lakes Ore Carrier, like the one on which I served
Picture credit—Steve Bosch

Rowboat that I built, Sitting on the Breakwater while Duck Hunting

My Wagemaker Racing Boat

One of Three Hydroplanes That I Raced.

CHAPTER 5 - THE BETTY J

TIME IS BUT A STREAM I GO FISHING IN

HENRY DAVID THOREAU

Around 1960, we purchased the fish tug, Betty J., a 50-foot-long steel boat with a single 671 GM diesel. My dad and I went to Erie, Pennsylvania, and bought the boat for $5,000. The boat was owned by a fleet owner, and it had become surplus to his needs. She had been laid up for over two years and needed work. The engine had not run, and the fuel tank contained fuel that was years old. The engine was new to me, so I had little knowledge of its parts or operation. I had run diesel boats in the Navy, but did not have to service them. To get the boat back to Lorain, we had to run it back a distance of 90 miles or more. After checking everything out as much as we could, we filled the tank with fuel, drained the filters, and checked the oil. Standard things to inspect were life jackets, flares, etc. It had a large, old-style depth sounder and an old ship-to-shore radio, neither of which worked that well, but we decided to go. The trip should take about twelve hours.

The lake was calm, and by the time we got away from the dock, it was getting dark. I took up a heading for Lorain. We had one old chart, but I set up a course for home. We ran at about 8 miles per hour, and estimated that we would be in the Lorain area by 6:00 am. At about 3:00 am, I awakened my dad and told him to hold the course I had set, and to wake me up when we got to Lorain. I fell fast asleep, and when I woke up, I looked out our port windows. I could see lights off of our port stern that looked like Lorain. I went up to the pilot house and asked my dad where in the hell we were. He said that we should be coming to Lorain soon—that the lake freighter up ahead was going there. I took another look out the port side, and hell, we were past Lorain. I could see the lights from the Ford plant. If my dad had followed that lake freighter, we would have ended up in Detroit.

I took the helm and turned around. At about 6 o'clock in the morning, we pulled into Lorain, docked the boat at Rieger and Warner's Fish Company, and went home. The next day, we went down to work on the boat to get it ready to fish with gill nets. We checked over the net-pulling machine, and got it running. We cleaned the boat where it was covered with dirt, old anchors, and junk. I thought that I may as well check out the engine and change the oil. I hit the starter; it ground and ground, but would not start. I decided to check the fuel filters and then go from there to decide the cause of it not starting. After opening the main fuel filter, I found that it was packed solid with sludge. When I opened the filter on the engine, it, too, had dirt. How we ever made that trip, I will never know! Although we put in new filters before we left Erie, the new ones were plugged. I bought more new filters to install, and the engine cranked over and started. We had to replace those filters three times before we cleared the tank. The old fuel had gone bad, and we just made it with the new fuel before she stopped. That was my introduction to diesel fuel filters. We now had a great little tug that ran real nice and handled great in the sea. We finished out the season and laid the boat up with great anticipation of the next spring. We now had a boat that we felt safe in, and it worked in almost any weather.

Spring came, and the weather was exceptionally cold for March 1st. The lake had heavy ice on it, and we had to hold off setting nets until the ice moved out, or the weather started a thaw. Finally, the lake had opened up, but the harbor still had heavy ice. The harbor tugs generally broke it up, but they were not running yet. So I and another tug, the *San Mar*, went out to start to break ice in order to be able to get out and set nets. The *San Mar* was a big tug with good power, and as we ran at the ice and ran up on it, the ice broke off. We made about 30 feet per hour. After we got about a hundred feet out past the river piers, the ice was over a foot thick. We ran at it, and the tug ended up on the ice with the bow out of the water. We sat and then backed off. This procedure we repeated until finally on one run, we went on the ice so far that we couldn't back off. I started to worry about what to do, when one of my crew members suggested, "Let's get out and use the jack." We got up forward to jack the bow up, and hoped that maybe she would come loose. I thought that the idea might work, so we got out on the ice which was thick enough to drive a tank. We put the jack under the bow, and we no more than got the front of the boat up a little, when she started to slide off of the ice. We ran and jumped on the rail to get back in the tug. We were all done breaking ice for that day! The *San Mar* broke through the ice and into the lake the next day, so we just followed her path that she made. We set nets in water that was about 34 degrees. A nor'easter hit the next day, and the nets were covered with ice. In springs like this one, we used ice buoys, which were long 2 x 4 poles tapered on one end, with a weight attached to the other. When the ice came up to them, it just shoved them under. When it moved off, they came up. It worked most of the time, but with heavy wind, the ice packed to twelve feet thick. We sometimes lost the nets. On this particular day, the wind shifted south, and the ice moved out. Before the ice had come back, the northeast wind created large waves and lots of current in the lake. When this happens, the nets take a beating. Well, we went out to make our first lift of the year. We found the ice poles and started the lifting machine. Up came the net full of dead shad. There were so many in the hundred foot net, that one the net filled a box. The shad were dead, bloated, and stunk, like you would not believe! We had 50 nets on a string, and each net was 140 feet long. One net to a box, meant 50 boxes of dead, rotten fish! They had been dead and lying on the bottom of the lake. The storm just washed them into the nets. The fish were so heavy in the net that the net was tearing, and the shad fell back in the water. All winter long, we worked to build these nets. Now, they were a stinking mess, full of junk, and all torn up!

As we continued to bring the nets aboard, I watched the rail on the opposite side of the tug to see how far we were down in the water from the weight we were taking aboard. I was kind of nervous that we may have too much weight here to safely bring aboard. When we got to about the 40th net, I looked at the bucking rail, and discovered that it was far too low in the water. I knew something had gone wrong. I ran to the engine room door to open it. My God, the engine room was half full of ice water! We had a bilge pump, which was a large pump with a gasoline motor on it. The water in the engine room was up to the mouth of the carburetor. The pump had a hand starting motor with a rope start. I jumped down into the engine room ice water and tried to start the pump. As I pulled the cord, some water was sucked up into the carburetor. I thought, "My God, we are done! I put the cord back on the motor and thought that I may as well forget it. The pump would not start. I left the engine room to call the Coast Guard.

We were ten miles out. Then something told me to have another go at that damn pump again. I jumped back in that freezing water, pulled the cord, and the motor started. It took about twenty minutes to pump her out, yet the water was still coming in the boat. Ice water was still flowing in from the stern. I got down low to look back into the stern, and I saw daylight coming in from a crack in the stern plate. I had backed into an ice floe on the way out and fractured that plate. The pump was holding well with the flooding, so we finished pulling nets. We headed toward the dock, and we dumped most of the shad in the nets back into the lake on the way there. We unloaded the nets and gear at the dock and took the tug over to the shipyard where they pulled it out of the water. The repair guys welded the plate, and we were back in business. It was not a good start for our new tug!

On one trip out to lift the nets, we rounded the lighthouse; the lake was rougher than hell with waves as high as six or seven feet, or more. I took a west heading to get through the breakers. All of a sudden a wave broke over the bow of the tug and hit the pilot house window, shoving it in. Water came into the pilothouse, hit the deck, and ran into the engine room. When the ice water hit the hot engine, steam rose and filled the pilothouse. The window broke loose. Hinge and glass came flying back and hit me in the face, cutting my cheek. Blood ran down my face. When the crew saw my face, they wanted to return to Lorain and come back tomorrow. I told them, "Like hell! We are out here, and this lake is not going to win." We went out four miles, pulled our nets, and had a good day.

At that time, walleyes were bringing in 10 cents a pound, and perch were 3 cents a pound off of the boat. I had to laugh one day when I was down at the dock, and a Pennsylvania boat, owned by the Smiley Fish Company in Erie was at the dock at Rieger and Warner's at the foot of 9th Street on the Black River. The tug was a beautiful 70 foot gill netter. Smiley had a very successful company and came up to Lorain in the spring to fish for walleyes. Joe Smiley was the captain, about 30 years old, a hard worker, and a nice kid. We joked a lot with Joe. On this particular day, I was up in the fish house, talking with Stacey Warner, one of the owners of the dock. Stacey told me to tell Joe that the price of perch was 3 cents a pound, and that they had increased the handling cost to 2 cents, which meant that Joe would get a penny a pound for his catch. The dock owners had an elevator-like hauling machine on rails to pull the fish up to the fish house from the tugs. I walked down the steep, wooden stairs, next to the lift and went over to Joe's tug. It was filled with about a thousand pounds of perch, and its crew of 4 or 5 guys were clearing them out of the net. Each fish had to be pulled out of the net, one at a time, because they were tangled up in the fine mesh of the net. Each fish had to have the twine cleared from its gill. The crew used, what we called, a picking hook, which had a small wooden handle with a bent hook on one end. The instrument is used to hook the fish in the eye and to pull them through the net. When someone breaks a bar of the twine to get the fish out, it can be heard. It was frowned on to break the bars, because the nets cost a lot of money. My dad used to cough or talk loudly when he broke a bar, so we didn't hear it, but we always knew.

Getting back to Joe Smiley—when I went down the steps to his tug, the crew was just finishing up getting the fish out of the nets and were about to put them on the lift to the fish house. I walked up to Joe and said, "Hey Joe! I got news for you!"

He said, "What's that?"

"Perch went to 3 cents a pound," I answered. We had been getting 5 cents.

"Oh well," he said

"That's not all," I told him. "They just told me that packing is 2 cents a pound!"

He looked at me, and without a blink, he told his crew to put the fish back in the nets. He was just kidding, but that was how the market played on the commercial fishermen.

To cut my overhead costs, later on, we bought a store up at 14th and Broadway in Lorain, and we shipped fish to State Fish in Cleveland. A guy, named Max, was the buyer. One time we came in with three thousand pounds of perch, which we unloaded on the floor of the store and iced them down. We had no boxes to put them in. Normally, the buyer sends the boxes, and the seller ships them back full of fish. Well, here we were with a pile of fish and no boxes. Perch were 3 cents a pound then. I called State Fish and got Max. I informed him that we had three thousand pounds of perch for him, and to send over some boxes for the fish. He paused and told me to put them in paper bags and hung up on me. We ended up selling them to a firm in Detroit for a penny a pound. The wholesalers had us over a barrel, and they controlled the price, which is why in early spring we got a good price for our catches, but as the season wore on, prices fell. Later on in the business, we commercial fishermen banded together and held back on our catches to get better prices.

When we first bought the fish tug, *Betty J.*, we started fishing for walleye mostly. As the year went by, we often headed down off of the Cleveland crib to fish for blues and whitefish. The bottom area around the Cleveland crib had a nice small gravel bottom where the blues and whitefish used to spawn every spring. It was a long run for us, but the fishing was excellent. Avon Point was the roughest part of the trip, but there was some protection until we got past the point. Coming home, the run used to take us about two and one half hours.

Often, in the summer, we had to run outside and fish the international line, where we encountered the Canadian tugs and got acquainted with some of the Canadian boats and captains. Their tugs were much larger than ours and much faster. The Canadian government was subsidizing the fishing fleet and worked with the fishermen to improve their boats and equipment. Many stories came to light in those days of fishermen drowning, tugs catching fire, and the crews perishing. On one such occasion, a 70-foot Canadian tug had a bottle of liquid gas in the pilothouse for heat. Somehow the bottle started to leak, and the tug caught fire. The crew was forced to climb up on the roof to seek shelter away from the heat. Soon, they had to jump in the water, because the fire had engulfed the entire tug. The water was ice cold, and they all perished.

The *Betty J.* was a 50-foot steel fishing tug that was entirely covered with a roof and steel sides. It had panels that were bolted on. After I got my masters' papers, we decided to remove the sides and get the tug certified for passengers for hire with the

U. S. Coast Guard. It was a lot of work and expense, because we had to secure a handrail all around the deck and bring the tug into compliance with all of the safety rules. We had to put 55-gallon drums of water to check the stability of the boat which would determine the number of people we could have aboard safely. The final result was 49 passengers and two crew members. After painting and rigging the tug, we were given the "green light" to run river and lake rides and to take fishing charters.

We had charters with various clubs from Lorain and Elyria. One club, the Canadian Club in Lorain, had an annual event. Big Don was the head of the fishing trips, and he was a great guy. He used to make all kinds of relish: a hot, a sweet, and one just right. He cooked up sauer kraut and sausage with that hot sauce. It made a great hit with the fishermen. They always had a keg of beer along, but never got drunk. They were a great bunch of guys who just had a great time.

It was always a problem to let people charter the boat and to bring drinks along. Beer was mostly okay, but they hid wine or booze and put it in pop bottles. On one trip we took to the Indians game in Cleveland, we had a bunch of people from Elyria. By the time I got to Avon Point, they were "half in the bag." I told my crew to keep an eye on them, because I sensed that they had liquor hidden somewhere. After we got to the dock in Cleveland, they went over to the game. The crew and I stayed aboard to clean up the boat. When the game ended, one of the guys returned to the boat and reported that the little guy with a derby hat on was so drunk that he got into a fight with some guy and fell all the way down the steps of the bleachers. At about the same time the rest of the passengers came back to the *Betty J.,* carrying the little guy, who was drunk as hell. I told my crew that when those guys weren't looking, to dump the beer over the side on the way home. We did pretty well for about an hour. We had just passed Avon Point, heading back to Lorain. All of a sudden, my crew came up to the pilothouse and told me that there was a fight in the back of the boat. I turned the helm over to my crew and ran to the stern. That little guy had a fork in his hand trying to stab another guy; the rest just stood there egging him on. I walked up, grabbed his arm, and took the fork away from him. I was pissed off and read the riot act to those guys, who were giving me a problem. I warned them to shape up, or I was going to dump them off of the boat. I went back up to the pilothouse, and we were about three miles from home when they started up fighting again. I took the tug, headed it right for the beach, and ran it up on the sand. I yelled for them to get the hell off of my boat. They asked me how in the hell they were going to get home. I answered that it was their problem. I went back up to the pilothouse, and just as I got there, the guy who was in charge of the trip came up and said, "Take us the rest of the way home, and I will see to it that these guys behave." I backed the tug off of the sand and ran home with no further problems. When we got to the dock, I told that bunch never to come back.

Another of my tribulations with drinking on board came with a trip that we had to Cedar Point with a bunch of guys and gals. It was a fun trip until we got there; then the problems started. I had docked the tug at the Cedar Point dock, where my crew and I decided to take a walk around the park after our passengers had left the boat. We no more than started out, when the Public Address system at the park blasts out, "Would the captain of the *Betty J.* come back to the dock?" We walked back, and there were two cops standing next to my boat. I walked up and one cop said, "Take this bunch and get them the hell out of here." I asked what was going on, and he informed me that one guy had fallen off the dock and fell into the tug. I walked over, looked, and there he was lying on the deck with blood all over the place. The other cop was trying to help him. I was informed that my passengers were all drunk, and that the park police were rounding them up and bringing them back to the boat. I had no idea that they had been drinking anything more than beer on the boat. They appeared to be okay when they left the boat to get on some rides to enjoy the day, but they sure got drunk in a hurry. We loaded them all aboard, and took them back to Lorain. I warned them never to come back. Of course, we had lots of good trips with fine people, and they enjoyed the river and lake rides and the fishing trips.

When I first bought the Betty J., it had a one-inch pipe in the pilot house that extended down to the reduction gear. It had a handle fashioned on the top end in the pilot house, so that when I pulled up, the gear was in reverse, when I pushed it down, the gear was in forward. Another charter story that I have to tell happened one day when we had 40 people aboard, and I was coming back to the dock. The tug had lots of power and was set up with a 6-71 GM for the main engine, with a 2.5 gear, so backing down to a stop was no problem. On this particular day, I was going to show off and come into the dock lively. Just ahead of me, at the dock, was a row of boats, getting bait. I didn't have much room to dock, but I had all of the confidence in the world that I could stop on a dime. I came in to dock, portside, at a good speed. I pulled up to the dock and pulled up on the pipe to hit reverse. The pipe came out of the hole in the pilot house deck. There I was, standing with a piece of pipe in my hand, while the tug was flying down the dock. I immediately realized that I had to do something quickly. I jumped out of the pilot house, ran down the deck, opened the engine room door, hopped in the engine room, grabbed the gear lever, and slammed it in reverse. I hit the throttle lever and stopped the tug. I then slammed the gear in neutral. When I came up on deck, the people on the tug looked at me, like what in the hell was that all about? The tug was sitting at the dock, while the crew set some lines out. The ride was over! That experience taught me a good lesson—always be ready for the unexpected, and don't try to show off with passengers aboard. Needless to say, I changed the pipe set up on the gear.

One thing I always changed or installed on all of my tugs and boats was a bilge high water alarm light on my dashboard. Many a tug has gone down, due to engine room flooding, because the skipper didn't know it until it was too late. Another good thing on the market is a bilge pump that pumps water, but not oil. I put it on a few of my tugs, and it saved my ass with the Coast Guard. Fuel lines leak, and oil gets in the bilge sometimes. That little gem can save the sailor lots of money, no matter how careful a person is, because it happens to the best of us. An example is when we had a 42-foot Stapleton with twin 6v-92s in it. We blew a gear and had gear oil in the bilge. We cleaned it up, disposed of the oil in a dockside drum, but there was still an oily film in the bilge. I had my son, Bobby, get some *Dawn* soap and clean it, again. He did, and had a 5-gallon bucket of soap and oil, which we took over to a dyke disposal area, near our dock and dumped it in a weeded area. Well some guy reported my son to the Coast Guard. Oh my God! The world came to an end! Forty Coast Guard people came running to the dock, made us dig up the area, and ship the dirt to a disposal site in China. I paid a good fine! The irony of this was that the disposal site was reserved for dredging material, which contained tons of oily waste from the river. Don't get me wrong; I support the Pollution Control Act 100 percent, but in some cases, there is overkill. A cup of oil in the water looks like the *Valdes* oil spill sometimes. For years, as harbormaster, I fought a losing battle with oil in the river from industry here. It wasn't until the EPA and the Coast Guard got into the act that things actually started to change. Our Black River, here in Lorain, wasn't much better than Cleveland's river that caught fire years ago. In those days, no one seemed to care much about pollution. Court records show that the cases I took to court, were either dismissed, or the parties paid a little fine for gallons of oil dumped in the river. The "Good Old Boys" were in charge back then!

On one occasion, a friend called and wanted me to go up to Sandusky Bay to break ice in the harbor, so that he could get his yacht over to his boathouse to lay it up for the winter. I asked him what the thickness of the ice was. He told me that it was about two inches. I got my dad, and we ran up to Sandusky Bay. It was December and cold as hell. We got to the bay at about 3:00 pm. The job took us about two hours to go from the shipping channel to his boathouse. When we got there, he paid me; we turned around, and headed back. It was getting dark, and we missed the channel marker and ran aground on a sandbar, just west of the channel. We finally got backed off of the bar and headed out, when the steering cable broke. It was the cable and the chain, and I had no way to repair it. I put my dad in the pilothouse, and I went back to sit with my feet on the quadrant to steer from there. We made it out of the channel and turned to the east. I left the stern and went up to the pilothouse to take a look at our course. The heading seemed good, so I returned to the stern. It was dark; I looked out the port light and saw a star right on the edge of the port. When I turned one way or the other, it disappeared. I had a star to direct my steering. For the next two hours that star was my compass. My dad was in the pilothouse as a lookout, and we made it all the way back to the Lorain lighthouse. After we rounded the lighthouse, I had to take orders from my dad to go to port, or go to starboard. We docked at Rieger and Warner's Fish Company dock with no trouble. What one can't do to improvise when one has to!

Another adventure occurred when we were gill netting, and it was early spring with lots of heavy fog. All the tugs sat at the dock, but the *Betty J.* was running every day, coming in with fish. None of the fishing tugs in those days had radar, GPS, Loran, or anything, but a compass. The other captains were going nuts, trying to figure out how I set and found my nets each day in such a heavy fog. It was literally impossible to see the bow of the tug. I knew I could find my way out of the harbor, and I knew if I could do that, I could find the lighthouse. We went out each day and ran from one side of the river to the other until we got out to the lighthouse. We dropped our net flag next to the lighthouse and set a course due west of the light. We did that for three days straight before the fog cleared, and we had to get out of there. No one ever did find out how we did it.

An old joke that went around the lake in those days was about an old fisherman named Soup Mouth Donley. He was fishing gill nets off of the old sailor's home down off of Erie, Pennsylvania. A sailor had died at the home, and Soup Mouth had taken a bearing on the flag to mark the spot where he had set his nets. The flag was at half mast, and Soup Mouth had to wait for another sailor to die in order to find his nets.

There were some really interesting people in those days. One fisherman that I had on my crew was a salty old guy, named Peanuts. He weighed about 110 pounds, soaking wet. He was 88 years old, and smoked four packs of cigarettes a day. My crew always wanted to take him and dunk him in the lake to wash him up. I don't think he ever took a bath. One day, we were out pulling nets, and we took some time to eat. We had a large coal stove on the tug, which we used to heat up a hot dog or sausage. Peanuts came back to the stove and put some sausage on the heater. He then walked over to the open door on the tug and dropped his pants to do his thing. He often did this, so we paid it no attention. He finished, but Peanuts didn't believe in toilet paper, so he just ran his hand down there and wiped it on his pants, and went to grab his sausage. He turned to my dad and asked if he wanted some. We all nearly busted a gut laughing. Although he was filthy, he was a great worker and a good fisherman. He swore a germ couldn't get near him. There is something that gets in your blood about the life of being out there on the lake every day in all weather and time. The work was hard, and sometimes it was an outright stinking mess, but for some reason you learn to love it.

Here is another amusing story. Years ago when we first started to set nets commercially, my dad and I had caught a bunch of walleyes, and they were only worth ten cents a pound. We used to take them up on Elyria Avenue and sell them three for a dollar. These were nice fish from 5 to 10 pounds. People sorted out the big ones for the three-fish-deal. Well, we had the boxes of fish in an open bed trailer and were going down Broadway. We were stopped by a cop who turned out to be Bep Fairis, a close friend of my dad's. He wanted to tell my dad about some meeting between the police and firemen. My dad was a fireman at the time. He stopped us and talked to my dad. I asked Bep if he wanted a couple of walleyes for supper. He told me, "Yeah, sure." He was driving his three-wheel motorcycle which had a small compartment on the back of the bike. I gave him two nice fish and warned him to ice and to clean them as soon as he got off work. Bep went back to the garage and parked his bike, forgetting the fish. He went on vacation. Soon after, the garage smelled like a garbage truck. The police hunted through the garage area and soon found the bike and the stinking fish. They argued about who was going to get the fish out of the bike. One brave soul held his nose as he drove the bike outside, where they hosed down the bike and removed the rotten fish. At first they through it was a prank, but when Bep returned from vacation, the case was solved. Bep was the recipient of many a joke after that. The case of the stinking fish was solved and soon faded away. Bep has long since gone on to the "Police Heaven in the

Sky." He was a great guy who was an outstanding police officer, a real ambassador of good will, and the city misses him dearly.

Just when we had the business going good the Portuguese and Italians came into the business. They had money and bought boats, nets, gear, licenses, and had the whole family on the boats working. Where we had been done at 1 or 2 pm, every day, and holding out on our catches, they used 500 to a thousand nets and fished from 6:00 am to 12 midnight. They caught 5 to 7 thousand pounds of fish a day, so the bottom fell out of the price again. Once I went over to their boat and asked why they didn't slow down and bring in half as much fish, and make just as much money. They looked at me and told me as much to mind my own business. I tried to explain the thing to them, and they came right out and explained that when they cleaned the fish out of here, they would go to another place and do the same thing.

Later on, we sold the *Betty J.* and quit fishing commercially.

Betty J #1—with Passengers, running up the Black River

Betty J #2—At the Dock at Riverside Park

Betty-J #3—Breaking Ice

CHAPTER 6 - FISHING TUGS

A BAD DAY'S FISHING IS BETTER
THAN A GOOD DAY AT WORK

ANONYMOUS

After about two years, I received a call from one of my old crew, Jim Plato. He wanted me to buy a 40 foot gill net boat from a guy in Sandusky. I agreed, and went up and got a nice little tug, but it had a gas engine. We gill netted with it, and had some good days. After the winter, we laid it up. When we were ready for spring fishing, I had built some more nets, and we started the season. We had ice in the harbor, and this little tug was not too good at breaking ice. We ran at the ice, slid up on it, but the tug wasn't heavy enough to break it down. We only had a hundred feet to go to be in open water where we could set out our nets. This boat, as I said before, had a gasoline engine, and we had a coal stove on deck for cold weather operation. Well, without thinking of what might happen, we backed up the tug about 200 feet and ran wide open at the ice, figuring the tug would run up far enough on the ice to break it down. We hit the ice, but the bow of the tug hit and stuck. It did not climb on the ice! I stood at the helm, and the coal stove broke loose from the deck behind me and rolled up and hit me in the ass. Smoke and fire was all over the deck, so I grabbed a fire extinguisher to put the fire out. Then we got a bucket and doused the stove which gave us a steam bath. We backed the tug out of the ice, went home, and thanked God that we did not blow up.

I was getting pretty tired of that small tug, and I began to look for something bigger. I heard of a tug for sale up in Port Sanilac, Michigan. My dad, Jim Plato, and I went up to see it. When we got to Port Sanilac to look up the owner, it was cold; it was February. After we found the guy and asked to see the tug, he took us down to the harbor and pointed to her. We looked out in the harbor, and there about 800 feet away sat the *William H. Jackaway*, frozen in the ice. The owner told us to go out and take a look at it, but I was familiar with this tug. A good friend of mine, Merle Jackaway, had operated her out of the fish house at Lorain each spring. We walked out on the ice and looked her over. She needed some paint and cleaning up, but was in great shape yet. We walked back to the beach, and I bought the 60 feet long, steel tug, with a great diesel engine for $5,000! We drove home, loaded up some gear, and returned to Michigan. We started her up, broke out of the ice and headed for home.

Running with the current, we made great time down to the head of Lake St. Clair, at Algonac. We docked and went up to a store for some food and coffee. The temperature was 4 degrees below zero. It hurt to be outside, because it was so cold. We had a full-sized furnace on the tug, and it was warm inside the tug, but outside it was brutal. We started down the river to the lake. When we got there, I called the Coast Guard to ask about ice conditions on the lake. They reported three inches of the stuff. When I got to the lake, the ice was 12 inches thick, so I turned around and returned to the dock at Algonac. I called the Coast Guard to see if there was an icebreaker around that could get us through the ice on the lake. The person on the phone asked who we were and what the name of the ship was. I told him that it was a tug. Well, they did not know that it was a fishing tug, and I was not about to tell them. In about four hours, a Coast Guard icebreaker showed up along side and screamed for us to get the hell out of the lake and back to port. The sailor told us that we had no right to be out in the lake in our boat. I told him that I had as much right to an icebreaker as an ore boat. I told him, "If you don't break ice for us, I will go by myself as far as I can!"

He shook his head, and said, "Come on." We did really well for about ten miles, right behind the icebreaker. The tug had chain and cable steering, and when ice hit the rudder, it was all we could do to hold the steering wheel in the center. It took both my crew and me to hold it. It was getting dark, and we were behind the icebreaker when he got stuck. I had the radio on and was in contact with the icebreaker. As soon as I saw that he was stuck, I hollered on the radio, "Don't back up!" It was too late. He was backing, and a large chunk of ice between him and me was shoving us backward. The stern hit the ice as we backed, and the ice hit the rudder, smashing the stern and breaking the rudder off. We were now dead in the water and sinking. The water poured into the stern where the rudder had been hit. I opened the stern manhole, and ice water streamed into the tug. I grabbed a raincoat and jammed it in the hole. I then took and 2 x 4 and jammed it over the raincoat, which slowed the water right down. My bilge pump, which ran from a belt from the engine, was keeping up with the leak. I called the icebreaker on the radio and informed them what was going on. It passed a towline over and started to tow us. As I recall, we had about twenty miles yet to go. The icebreaker was unable to back up. It had to increase power to plow through the ice. We were clipping along at a nice speed, when I was informed that the other ship had blown an engine. We made it to Detroit at about six in the morning. It was raining and freezing; everything was ice. The Coast Guard captain cut me loose at the shipyard, and I was hauled out to repair the damage. The cutter captain took off, and didn't say goodbye. Later on in the story we meet again, but that's another chapter in my life.

The *William H. Jackaway* was a great tug and a great sea boat. We got a dock down at the Riverside Park, and as harbormaster, the city was okay with it, because I did use the tug for city jobs. On one occasion, the Port Authority made up a break wall, using eight hundred tires lashed together. The plan was to make a break water over at the east side of the river, near the mile-long pier, so that they could build a marina there. The Port Authority made up these floating tires at 9th Street on the Black River, and did so in sections. They had no way to get them out into the harbor; therefore, I volunteered to use my tug to pull them out there. On the first section of tires, I used a tow from the front of the tires, but the tow line was hard to control, and it was hard to get them through the bridge and out into the harbor. It seemed as though the tires bogged down, as we towed. The sections were about 300 feet long by 60 feet wide, so on the second trip, I decided to put my bow up to the center of the tire section, and to push it, which turned out to be the answer. Towing it spread the tires out; pushing it compressed them and made the tow much easier. I don't recall how many sections I towed, but I think it was 5. The last section of tires had been sitting in the river for some time, before I towed them over to the area where they were to be assembled for the break water to protect a marina and dock boats. The rubber tire break wall was supposed to calm the water and to make a safe haven for boats to dock. I was on my last section and just cleared the river pier light. All of a sudden I hit something with my prop and started to get a lot of vibration.

Thankfully, I had the section of tires near their destination. It appeared that a large tree limb was forced under the tires. As I pushed them, the limb hit my prop. The rudder seemed to be jammed somehow. Anyway, I finished the job and took the tug over to the shipyard to have it pulled out of the water. The shaft was bent; the prop was bent; the rudder had to be taken off, and the rudder-packing gland had to be rewelded. Since there were no lifts big enough to handle a sixty-foot tug around at that time, I had to go to the shipyard with all of my work. This particular job cost me over $4,000, which I paid for out of my own pocket. I didn't even ask the city for it. I just paid it, and acted as though it was my contribution to the project. I never even got a "thank-you" from the Port Authority. I was laid up at the shipyard for about a week. I had the workers paint the bottom while it was in the yard, which cost an extra thousand. They threw in an extra can of paint for me.

Without warning, I was accused of using my job as harbormaster for favors from the yard. The jealous "wannabes" were at it again! From time to time, I did do jobs diving for the shipyard and got to know the manager and yard foreman really well. They always treated me well, and I never overlooked a violation because of that. In fact, I did take them to court on an oil spill.

On one diving job, the guys in the yard had dropped a large pump into the river and needed a diver to attach a line, so that they could pull it out. I went down to the river and found that the pump had been dropped right into the center of the channel. It was very cold weather, and they showed me approximately where the pump was. It was a free dive, meaning no air line, just a tank and mask. The water was like ink; I could not see an inch ahead of me. I dove about 30 feet deep, and as luck would have it, I found the pump right away. The scary thing was that I was right inside of it. I had swum into the mouth of this huge pump. My heart started to beat a little faster and harder, as I felt my way round the side of the opening. I said to myself, "Calm down! You have lots of air left. You got in here somehow; just keep feeling your way around." Then I remembered that I had a line with me. I just followed it out, and yanked on the line to send down a cable. I shackled the cable to the pump and left the water. They pulled the pump up with a large crane.

My next job for the shipyard was to find a large cribbing that had stuck under a 500 yard mid body at the yard, when they flooded the dry-dock. The ship had floated out and moored to the south wall at the shipyard near the launch dock. It was winter; ice was on the river. The shipyard called me to ask if I would take the job. I accepted. I got my wet suit, my dry suit, my hookah outfit and went down to the dock. There was a guy there to handle my lines. I dressed and got on the dive barge. We started about a hundred feet from the north end of the ship's mid body, about where the section of timber cribbing should have been. Again, these jobs were always in murky water, so that I couldn't see my hand in front of my faceplate. I dove in, and the first effect of the ice water chilled me. When my body heat started to be contained by my suit, I became somewhat warm. The mid body had been built in Germany and shipped over to the states, as I understood it. I started to feel my way long the bottom of the ship, using the welded seams as a guide. The welders had done such a good job that it was difficult to keep on a line by feeling. I came out, took off my gloves, and went back down. When I got to what I guessed was the center of the beam, I turned right, then went south, using the welds as a guide. The ship was about fifty-five feet wide, so it was a long process. It was a lot easier to feel the welds with my bare hands, but now they were getting numb. I had only covered about a hundred feet, when suddenly I heard a thump. The timber had shifted just enough for me to hear it bump the bottom of the hull. It was close by, so I kept going. Immediately, I heard it again, and it sounded as if it was really close now. I kept going ahead and bumped by head on the timber, so I jerked on the tag line that I had bent on to my belt. The tender on the raft sent me a tow line, which I tied onto the cribbing. My job was done! I came out from under the ship before the shipyard launch pulled the cribbing free. Everyone was happy. I made $500 to do the job, and saved the shipyard thousands.

Some time later I received a call from a marine contractor doing a job on the Miller Road sewer. I went out, and he wanted me to go out in the lake and block off the outlet end of the sewer pipe with a cap and bolt it on. They had a tank of welding air there, and I hooked it up to my mask. Off we went, about 500 feet out from shore. I dove down, taking the cap with me. On this job, I had visibility to about twenty feet. As soon as I got to the bottom, I noticed that the area around the end of the pipe was white as snow. Whatever came out of the pipe was covering the lake in this area. I worked for about fifteen or twenty minutes, put the cap on, and they pumped the sewer dry. After the contractor completed the job, I had to go out to take the cap off. They paid me, but I frequently wondered about that white stuff because it smelled terrible, and so did I! My diving suit fell apart, so I threw it away. I had that junk on my skin for a week afterwards.

This section would not be complete without some mention of my friend, Bill Virgin, a local iron worker and commercial diver. Bill was a man who was tough as hell, and took no shit from anyone. Yet, once I got to know him, he was truly a great guy! When I became harbormaster, I appointed Bill as part of my team for any emergencies in the port. I had guys who were good with explosives and guys who were good at about any other waterfront job. Politics and time destroyed that project. My last dive job was not a job at all, but a treasure hunt. I had built an underwater sled and had bought a trap net boat, *The Mermaid*, from Cleveland. I had my dad run the boat, while I held on to the sled. We went out to the sand bar, five miles out, to look for a sunken ship. I had done this before on several occasions, but found nothing. Dave Boley, a diver, convinced me that there was a fortune to be found out in the lake. He said, "It's there; all you have to do is find it." I can say definitively that I saw more of that sand bar bottom than any man alive. For two days, my dad dragged me around that bar, and all I saw was sand. If you have ever seen pictures of the Sahara Desert, that is how the sand down there looked. At times, there are small pebbles and soft mud and sand, but on the bar itself, it is a barren stretch of sand, broken only by a clam trail once in a while. My chances of finding a ship full of copper bars ended. I gave up! Legend has it that that ship is still out there, somewhere.

I often hired guys to make fishermen out of them, but only one or two out of a hundred actually stayed with it. One really had to love the lake and the life we lived. Some days, such as I have described earlier in this book, a person worked all day and made nothing. The crew worked on shares; if we caught no fish, we made no money. The thing that kept us going was the anticipation each day of how many fish we would catch. When the nets came up loaded with fish, everyone sang and danced around on the tug. When the nets came up empty, and that happened a lot due to slime and/or weather, nobody said anything. Early in the spring, when the water was cold, we used to get cold water slime on the nets. When that happened, the fish lead on the net and did not try to get through it. After running for about two hours in rough weather, we pulled the nets, only to find them to be empty or worse yet, destroyed by a storm, which is disheartening. We worked until our hands ached from stringing nets all winter, and the first time that they were set, they were destroyed. A commercial fisherman learns to live with that, and accepts it as a challenge. Friend or foe, is the lake, and we fought to keep it from beating us. There were other days that were more enlightening and funny, however.

On one trip down off of the Cleveland crib, it was late in the fall. It had been snowing and blowing hard when we got down to the nets. The snow picked up to a point, where we could hardly see a half mile ahead. We were about to pull up the buoy, and there was a break in the snow. I saw something off in the distance that looked like a small boat. I told the crew that I thought I saw something out that there looked like a small boat. They came up to the pilot house and told me that they saw nothing out there, so I just went up to our buoy, thinking I was seeing things. Sometimes, with fog or heavy snow, a person has this happen, as he strains to see through the limited visibility. Yet, once again, I saw something out there. I could not imagine anyone being out this far in the lake at this time of the year in a small boat. But who knows, weirder things than that have happened! I told the crew to hold off that I was going to take another look. It was snowing hard, so I could not see very far. I steered out in the direction of where I had thought the boat was. In an instant, we came out of the snow and there sat a 14 foot open boat with two guys in it. I pulled up along side of them, and they acted as though they were frozen. We got them aboard and sat them next to our stove. They were two old farts who explained to us how they were fishing about a half mile off of the wall in Cleveland. Their anchor had broken loose, and when they tried to start the engine, it would not start. We took their little boat in tow and ran them in to the ramps and dropped them off. As they left, they said, "We will never complain about commercial fishermen again in our lives. You saved our lives; thanks. We will tell the Coast Guard and the news media about this." Of course, we never again heard a single word about this situation.

You may not believe this story, but it is true! We were on another trip to the Cleveland crib, fishing for whitefish. It was a calm, nice day in the fall—a little cold, but nice. As we pulled nets, we cleared them of scrap fish, which we dumped back into the lake. The seagulls were just about climbing in the boat to get at the dead fish that we were dumping. I called one of my crew over to the pilot house and told him to take the dip net and dip up a few of those gulls. He looked at me as though I was nuts. I had to

Repeat, "Get the dip net, and catch me some seagulls."

"What in the hell do you want with them damn things?" he asked.

"Don't worry about it; just get 'em!" I responded.

Well, he dipped up six gulls and said, "There ya are cap; have fun!"

I walked back to the stern of the tug where we had a large steel vat full of water, which we used to dye our nets from time to time, depending on the water quality. The fish sometimes lead on the nets. When a fisherman dyes them different colors, the fish try to go through the nets and get caught.

I had other ideas. The gulls that he had dipped up for me were running around the tug, so I caught them and took them over to the water vat and dyed them. They were pink! When they dried out, we let them go. A week later, the Cleveland newspaper had a small article about someone who had seen a flamingo off of Cleveland. They were excited about that, because another guy had seen one as well. We laughed until our sides hurt when we read the story.

There were always stories about the lake and the business. Some are believable, while at others, we just shook our heads. Here is one about the early days and Tom Todd, who owned a boathouse on the river, near the old bridge. Tom, as the legend goes, was a giant of a man and strong as an ox. He was a commercial fisherman. One day he was carrying a box of lead, which must have weighed over 200 pounds, to make weights for his nets. A guy stopped to talk with Tom for over an hour. What is ironic about it was that Tom never set the box of lead down. Another story about Tom was that he was arrested in Canada for being over the International Line. They took his nets, all of his fish, and told him never to return. He came home, and later found out what the Canadian authorities had done with his nets. They were in ten boxes over in Wheatley in a shanty. Tom made plans to get his nets back. On the first moonless night, he sailed over to Wheatley. No one had seen him come into the harbor, so he walked up to the shanty and knocked on the door. A watchman came to the door half asleep. Tom befriended the guy, because Tom had brought a bottle of home brew with him. After the watchman became drunk, Tom loaded his nets on his boat and sailed back to Lorain.

In 1975, there was a more recent case of a commercial fisherman going over the limits of the law. He was a fishing tug owner who was noted for his quick temper. As captain of his tug, he "ruled the roost," so to speak. Anyway, the wholesalers used every opportunity to beat us out of a nickel. This guy got fed up with it. He had come in with a load of fish, and the truck came down from the wholesaler to pick up the fish. The dealer had not paid for the last three loads that the fisherman had sent him. The wholesaler was behind on paying the guy. The dealer parked the truck next to the tug to load the fish. The captain asked for his check that they were supposed to bring. The captain said, "No fish without a check." They told him to keep his fish that they would get fish somewhere else. Before they could leave, the skipper ran to his pilot house to get a shotgun. He ran up to the truck and shot out all four tires. We were just coming into the river from out in the lake and saw the whole thing. Later on he came up to our tug and said, "I got my money, and they agreed to pay me every time I came in to ship the fish to them!" So as they say, "The squeaky wheel gets the grease," or more like, "The shotgun gets their attention."

Later on, we added another gill net tug, *The Ronald E.*, a sixty foot steel tug with twin 3-71 GM diesels. My faithful crew member, Jim Plato, and I went to Dunkirk, New York and looked at this tug for sale. It had twin engines, and no matter what we did, they would not run. Yet, it was a nice tug, and I bought it for $5,000. We went home and got the *Jackaway*, now named the Betty J. III. There was a reason that I named most of my boats the Betty J. You see, I had about 300 nets with 10,000 lead weights on them. They were stamped "Betty J.," so rather than restamp all the lead weights with the different names of our tugs; we solved the problem by naming each new boat the same as the original. What was funny about that, was the guys used to call Virginia, my wife, Betty. Anyway, getting back to my story, we ran down to Dunkirk, New York, with the Betty J III, took the new boat in tow, and headed home to Lorain. Everything went well until we got off at Cleveland, when an ocean boat came flying out of there, and damn near ran over our towline. We pulled into Lorain, and I worked on the engines all day, trying to get them started. No good, they were shot, so I went up to the bus company and bought two busses that had 6-71 engines in them. We took them and rebuilt them to marine specifications. These were very versatile engines that can be adapted to almost any application. We tore the 3-71 engines out of the tug, and installed the 6-71 engines, putting straight pipes on them. They sounded like ab-29 coming, and I only gained about 4 miles per hour with the bigger motors.

I hired a captain and crew, and we now had a fleet with two boats. I don't recall when we added the third boat, but we had bought a trap net boat, *The Mermaid,* and ran trap nets also. When I bought the trap net boat, I inherited a ton of equipment. There were three trap net trucks, 300 trap nets, 200 trap net anchors, and the equipment was all over in the fields in Cleveland. There was a dock off of the main channel over there, and a barn filled with the old trap nets, trucks, and gear. We salvaged one truck and loaded as much stuff as we could and brought it home. The rest could have been ours, but it needed lots of work to salvage, and I did not have the help or the time to do it. Trap netting was new to me, so I hired a guy to run the trap net boat. It was interesting work, but the nets we had were too big. Most of them were 30 foot nets, and they fish top and bottom in 30 feet of water. We also had some small trap nets that were ten footers, with which we fished on the beach off of Martin's Run. We had good hauls of walleye, Coho, and catfish in them. Because we had no market for Coho, we released them. How matter how we tried to dip them out gently to put them back in the water, they went into shock and died, sinking tail first. The nets were old and tore easily. In one storm on July 4th, we lost all of our nets off of Huntington Park. There wasn't even a buoy left; they were destroyed. That area had produced some of the nicest perch we ever caught. It was the best place to fish, but it wasn't long before the Italians found the place and took over.

There was one guy, I kind of liked who had a sense of humor and treated us local guys well. He was an Italian guy, named Carlos, and we got along together well. My close friend, another gill netter, named Ziggy, worked with me, and we told each other where the fish were. We set up a code, and if I said the fishing was no good, it meant that it was great! If I said that it was good, that meant it was bad. We went on like this for quite a long while. One day, I called Ziggy on the radio to tell him no good, no fish, bad day. Ziggy came back to me with an okay. Instantly, Carlos came on the radio and said, I know you, Bobby. You say no good; that means good." He had broken our secret code. The next day, Carlos was on our tail and continued every day from then on. We soon found out that he was a great guy and we shared our information freely.

At about this time, things were going downhill. The sport fishermen were mad! To some extent, I didn't blame them. The out-of-country fishermen had come in with so many nets that it was hard for the sport fishermen to ignore them. Their net flags were starting to cover the lake, and some more aggressive sport fishermen took the law into their own hands, and started to raid the nets and cut the buoys. After that, they began to cut up the nets. There was nothing more disheartening than to go out and to see my nets all cut up and floating on the surface of the water. There were times that I sat in the pilot house and cried like a baby.

I loved people and wanted to be friends with everyone, yet, here was a person who did not know me at all, and hated me for being a commercial fisherman. It got worse and worse. One day in 1979, I believe, the ODNR (Ohio Department of Natural Resources) agreed with the sport fishing interests and passed a law to ban gill nets. At fifty-five years old, I was out of a job, with over $200,000 worth of equipment and boats that were worth nothing now. The nets, we had, were junk. We sold the fish house cheaply. The boats were eventually sold, but we took a lost; and we were paid off by the state in accordance with how big "a hog one was." The people, who caught the most fish, received the most money. At that time it seemed like a fair deal, but looking back, they took away my life, and sadly no other young man will ever get a chance to have the life that I did. It was a life that sport fishermen will never understand. It gets in your blood, just as sport fishing does, but it becomes a way of life, and a chance to be hear the God-given elements. You feel a closeness to your maker that no other job offers. You talk to Him every day, asking why, sometimes, and saying thanks, at other times. It is too bad that we all cannot experience and share that love of our lake. It is a magnet that attracts your heart and soul. Thank you, God, for giving me that chance to be with You. In 1980, we sold the fish house, the boats, and the equipment, and left the commercial fishing business. Yes, I miss it!

Betty-J#1 Docked at Muny Pier with
Canadian Club passengers

My Trap Net Tug, *The Mermaid,*—Nice Tug!

Me, in My Harbormaster Uniform

Inside the *Betty-J* Fish Tug with My Wife Virginia, My Son, Bob, and My Dad, Removing Fish from Nets.

Our 65-Ft. Gill Net Tug—*Ronald-E* at the Shipyard

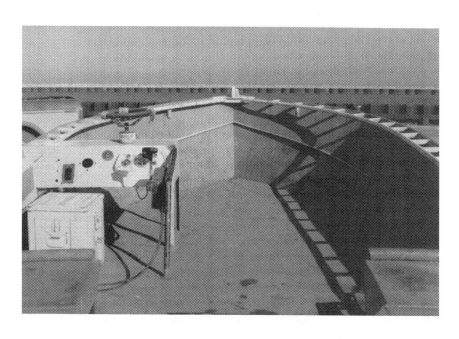

My Son, Bob's Small Gill Net Boat

CHAPTER 7 VACATIONS

THE CURE FOR ANYTHING IS SALT WATER - SWEAT, TEARS, OR THE SEA.

ISAK DINESEN

In earlier years, for vacations, we went down to Fort Myers, Florida and visited my parents who had moved there and bought a home in a mobile home park, Mobile Manor on McGregor Blvd. When we used to go there, we stayed with my folks in the park. Dale Shardon, a close friend of my dad, was also a home owner in the park. They all liked to golf. Dale was a retired fire chief from here in Lorain, and my dad was a retired fireman. Dale was a great guy, and he and Don McGrady, the assistant chief were all good friends of my dad and me. Dale talked my dad and me into going golfing while I was there in Fort Myers.

I had started to golf, and during my first trip out, I shot a 41 for nine holes. That was the first time I ever had a club in my hand. As I played on the course at home with guys from the Chamber of Commerce, and a few local lawyers, they convinced me that if I got a pair of golf shoes, gloves, and better clubs, I could be on the tournament swing in no time. Well, I got the gloves, the shoes, and the clubs, and my game went up to 49 and 50 for 9 holes. Hell, I couldn't hit a bull in the ass with that little golf ball now.

Back at Fort Myers, my dad and Dale got me out on the golf course, and invited a 91-year-old guy to play along with us. When we picked him up at his home, I did not think he would make it to the car, let alone play golf! We got to the course and started to play. I teed off first. I hit a nice shot down the middle of the fairway and felt pretty good about that. My dad, Dale, and the old guy teed off. My ball was the shortest drive of all. To make a long story short, I got so pissed off that by the time we got to the sixth tee, I took my clubs and sold them to Dale for $100. I had just bought those clubs for $350.00! I took off my shoes, which were the black and white spectator type, and gave them to Dale also. I just felt that if a 91-year-old guy could be me now, I may as well quit. I never played golf again—what a frustrating game!

When we went down to see my parents in Florida again, it was in the summer, around August. It was so hot down there that our feet burned right through our shoes when we walked on the pavement.

At one point in our earlier travels, we had gone to Miami Beach, after being married for only a few years. That year we decided to go back there on vacation. We bought a new Buick convertible and drove all the way down to Florida, using Route A-1A, through the coastal towns and across bays on ferries. By the time that we pulled into Miami Beach, we were exhausted. It was getting dark, and all of the lights were on in Collins Avenue. We just sat in the car with our mouths opened, driving past these gorgeous hotels and night clubs with limos driving guests into them. My wife and I looked like a couple of rag dolls. I was unshaven, and Virginia's hair was a mess. We neared the Thunderbird Motel, but next door was the Ocean Shores Motel, where we had planned to spend the night. We drove in and went into the office. It was a small place, compared to the others, but we fell in love with it. Our room was on the first floor, right at the ocean's edge. We heard the waves breaking at night which was very soothing to us. The motel had a nice pool and a little restaurant in the front which seated about 25 people. We enjoyed our stays there and returned to it on three or four more occasions in the winter. Have you ever noticed that nothing ever stays the same?

When we went back one year, the Ocean Shores was gone; the Golden Nugget had bought it out, so we went back to Fort Myers.

On another trip down to Florida, we saw the bare hull of a large fiberglass boat that had just been launched. At first glance, it looked to be about a hundred feet long. Without a deck or a house on it, it looked enormous. It was being built for use as a head boat. That year was 1971, and ironically, it was the *Miss Majestic* that we would buy later in 1981.

Virginia and I had been married for 35 years by 1981, and we had two children: a son, Bob, Jr., and a daughter Carol. I was fifty-five years old, and out of a job. Our fishing business had been shut down by the State. Both kids were happy and great. Bob was married with three kids, and Carol was married with a little girl. We now had four grandkids. My life had been destroyed, and I was now taken away from my beloved lake.

As a diversion from my troubles, we drove down to Fort Myers and went fishing on a 40 foot Stapleton, and I fell in love with it. It was fifteen feet wide, with twin engines. It was fast and comfortable, so we decided that the next time we came down that we would bring our 26 foot Penyan with us.

That winter, we hooked up the trailer, put my grandkids, son, and his wife in the back of the pickup and drove to Fort Myers. It was a gruesome trip, like walking on egg shells through all of that traffic, pulling a trailer with a boat that far. We made it, and stayed at Fort Myers Beach. We had our own dock behind the motel. The first night there, it started to rained, and it rained, and it rained buckets and buckets. The next morning, I went out to check the boat, which was all but sunk. The rain had filled it up, so I got the bilge pump working and emptied it out, but it started to rain again. This time the rain lasted three days in a row. Our vacation was being washed away! We stayed for a week, left, and went home—boat and all.

On another occasion, my son and I flew down to Fort Myers and bought a commercial fishing boat. It was what they called a mullet boat. We bought some nets and started to catch mullet for the smokehouse. Wholesalers took these fish and smoked them. They were delicious! Talk about two guys who didn't know what in the hell they were doing, that was Bobby and me. The ideas was when we spotted a school of mullet, we were to surround the whole school with a net. Well we spotted a school of the fish, ran the net around them, but they refused to go into the net. My son jumped in and started to chase the mullets into the net. As our luck would have it, we set the net on an oyster bed with which contained sharp, razor-like shells. Bob took one step and jumped back into the boat. His feet were all cut up! When he hopped in the water, the fish jumped over the net and left. Our first attempt at mullet fishing was a disaster!

We thought that there must be some easier fish to catch. After all, we weren't rookies. We had fished commercially at home, so went after pompano. We found out that we had to catch them at night. We loaded up the net in the boat and left the dock to go out into the gulf. Bob asked, "Don't you think we should ask someone what a pompano looks like?"

I answered, "By God, you're right. How in the hell are going to know what they are if we don't know what they look like?"

We stopped at the fish house dock and walked up to a place, when a guy came out to ask us if we needed ice. We asked how much, and he said, "You're going out to catch us some fish, aren't you?" We looked at each other, and told him that we were. He went into the building and came out with a large box of ice. He asked, "Is that enough?" I told him that it was, and again I asked him how much we owed him.

He said, "Are you kidding me? It's free! Are you guys commercial? I haven't seen you here before."

I told him that we were pompano fishermen, and he kind of grunted and walked away. I looked at Bob and told him to ask what a pompano looks like. He said, "Hell no, you ask!" We stood there trying to get enough nerve to go in and ask one of the old-time fishermen. Finally, I mustered up some bravery, walked up to a guy, and said, "Tell me something. What does a pompano look like?" He asked, "What?" I repeated, and he started to laugh, and asked, "Are you serious?" I told him the story of buying the boat and all the gear. He turned out to be a good sport. He took us into the fish house to show us a pompano. He then gave us some pointers in catching them.

We left the fish house and went out into the gulf. We had a moon out which was supposed to be a good time for pompano. We set the net out, just as we had done in Ohio, and waited. At about midnight, we started to pull the net up. I took the side with the corks, and Bobby had the side with the leads. We no more than started pulling the net, when my son screamed, "Ouch! Ouch!" I asked him what in the hell was the matter. He told me that something was biting him. We couldn't see what it was because it was dark! We were pulling a net up with stuff in it that we couldn't see. After a while, Bob asked me to switch sides with him, so I agreed. I told him that we only had another fifty feet or so to go. He said, "Like Hell! I quit! I'm getting all bitten up, and it hurts!" I told him to get out of the way, and I took the lead line. Something got a hold of my finger and would not let go. Bob was standing there laughing his ass off, while I am screaming like a banshee. Here we are, the great pompano hunters, getting bitten up like mad and we can not see what is biting us!

We put the net in the bottom of the boat and went into the dock to tie up and go home. We figured that the next morning we would see what we had caught. We came down to the dock at dawn and looked in the boat. There was a net full of blue crabs. We were able to get them out of the net, because we could see them in the daylight and avoid their pinchers. We must have had a hundred of the damn things, so we took them up to my dad's place. His next door neighbor came over to see what we had. We asked him if he wanted the crabs. Boy! He grabbed them and ran home. We didn't know any better, but they were really good to eat, and we gave them away. Afterwards, the neighbor fixed some and brought them over for us to try. I didn't like them! That was the end of our commercial fishing in Fort Myers, for we sold the boat and nets to some guys who knew what they were doing.

From then on, our trips there were for visiting my parents and sport fishing. We had some great times fishing for tarpon under the Sanibel Bridge at night. That is exciting fishing! The channel through the bridge is about a hundred feet wide with a row of timber piling leading into the bridge channel. If a person gets under the bridge without the operator seeing him or her, when the tide slacks, around midnight, the place just swarms with fish: big fish, small fish, skinny fish, fat fish—all kinds. First, the lady fish come up, then the Snook, then the tarpon. It is non-stop action. Once the operator of the bridge spots someone—he or she is done, but until he does—Wow!

The lady fish are about thirty inches long and skinny. They jump when hooked, and they actually jump in and out of the boat. It is funny and fun! Then the Snook hit, and they look something like a walleye, but certainly don't act like a walleye. If a person hooks into a thirty-inch Snook, he or she is in for a battle! One needs some good line and a good rod, because these fish do not quit! If a person is close to the pilings, the fish like to play, "Let's-go-around-the-piling" a few times. Next, the monsters, the tarpon, show up right next to the boat and are fearless. When a hundred pound tarpon rolls right beside the boat at night, a fisherman can not help but to be impressed! They remind me of a giant shiner minnow. Here again, these things have no quit! A fisherman can cast spoons for them, but the best luck we have had was using live bait, a small mullet—dead or alive.

I had a hundred pound tarpon on once, and just as he had hooked up, we were under the Sanibel Bridge. A yacht came through the bridge and my tarpon jumped on the other side of the channel. The yacht just came coming, so I jumped on top of the piling and held the pole way up in the air. The boat ran under my line and kept going. My fish took off and damn near pulled me off the piling! I jumped back down in the boat, while the bridge operator hollered at us to get the hell out of there. I cranked the drag down and started to hurry up to get the fish in to the boat. Big mistake! The tarpon took a long run and broke a hundred pound swivel. Away he went!

One other time, we sat along side the bridge, and my dad had a large, ocean reel and rod baited with a whole mullet. We were about sixty feet away from the bridge wall, when a tarpon grabbed his line and took off. Dad must have tightened the drag down all the way, because his rod was bent totally under the boat. He stood, holding that rod with all the strength he could muster. He did not give that fish an inch. Instantly, that fish, the big tarpon, came up and jumped about five feet out of the water, next to the bridge concrete. He left he imprint of his body right on the bridge wall. The line broke, and the fish is probably still going, I think! We laughed for an hour afterwards. Our trips South were filled with family fun, and we hated it when we had to leave. Our summer vacations ended when we went out of the commercial fishing business.

CHAPTER 8 - MISS MAJESTIC

MANY MEN GO FISHING ALL OF THEIR LIVES WITHOUT KNOWING THAT IT IS NOT FISH THEY ARE AFTER

HENRY DAVID THOREAU

In 1981, I started to talk with an owner of a large fiberglass boat that was for sale in Key Largo, Florida. He wanted $195,000 for the boat, but I offered him $150,000, which was turned down. I gave up on buying such an expensive boat, but I wanted to buy something nice for Lorain—something that I could get a lot of fishermen on, and yet take charter rides. *The Miss Majestic* was a beautiful boat, 72-feet long with a 19 foot beam. She was U.S.C.G. certified for 78 passengers. The boat had two 12-v 71 GM diesels at 450 horsepower each. The pilot house was topside and loaded with electronics. When we had been down at the Keys, I saw the boat. I went aboard her to look her over. My wife just stood on the dock and shook her head. She asked, "What in the hell do you want with that monstrosity?" That's the word she used! My son said, "Dad that is nothing but work!" I fell in love with that boat. As it turned out, this was the huge hull I saw being built in 1971, over in Fort Myers. I visualized how it would look completely cleaned up and painted. I just could not get the boat out of my mind. I drove my wife nuts. "Put that money in the bank! Forget about it," she begged, but I didn't hear her. I wanted that boat! How proud I would be to come into Lorain with such a beautiful thing! How much fun we could have taking 50 or 60 guys and gals fishing, and for rides!

We came home, and I, again, contacted Jerry, one owner. He owned the boat with a guy, named Tom. Jerry was ready to sell; Tom was not. I offered them $175,000, which they turned down. About a month later, I received a call from Jerry. He and Tom had run to Cuba, picked up a group of Cubans, and brought them into Miami with the blessing of the government. Over some mix-up, they were charged with bringing the group in illegally, and they were afraid that their boat would be taken away. I was not aware of the situation at the time, but Jerry said, "If you want the boat, we will sell it for $195,000.

I went to the bank to ask what I could do. First they bank wanted a survey of the public to see if it was feasible to invest in the boat. I had the Port Authority run a questionnaire to see how Lorain felt. It went over big! The bank gave me a $150,000 loan at 19 percent interest. As I remember it, the payments were about $2,500 a month. We had a secured loan, a SMBL. I gambled that the interest would come down, and I was right!

Once the papers were finalized, the *Miss Majestic* now our property. Jerry Theiss, the previous owner, my dad, and I were going to take her to see her new home on Lake Erie. We got underway from Key Largo at 5:55 in the morning. My captain's log for that odyssey can be found in the epilog in the back of the book

Lots of local business men were predicting that I would lose my shirt, but I proved that if a person wanted something badly enough, any odds can be overcome. It was hard work! My wife and I spent lots of days on the boat, and then we ran night trips as well. We made the payments, but it was rough. Many a day, we went to bed at 11 or 12 o'clock, and were up at 5:00 am to start all over.

The fishing trips were doing great, but our big mistake was that we were too cheap on our price. We started out at $15 each. The fishing was so good that we could have gotten $20 to $25 each, with no trouble, but we felt with the capacity of 60 or 70 guys, that $15 was enough. We gave the fishermen a big break on price, because we had lots of old timers and ladies who just loved that boat. People from all over the country came to us to fish. Our trips to McGarvey's Restaurant, in Vermilion, were packed, with a full load coming home at night. Sometimes the lake was rough with the wind on our bow. People used to stand in the bow and get wet from the spray, but they loved it!

I was always worried that some little old lady was going to come up to the pilot house to hit me with her handbag when she got wet, but it never happened. The passengers just loved the trips.

Eventually I started to run into Cleveland for the air shows, and baseball and football games. We worked hard at it, and made the payments—never late on one. Sometimes it was a bad situation, going and coming home at night with so much boat traffic, but we got by. We had the boat running every day that we were able, due to weather conditions, as you can imagine. One bunch quit us for canceling a trip. The lake was rough, but they didn't believe me. We took no chances because safety was always our first consideration. For some trips we had live music, with an organ or piano playing for the passengers.

The walleye fishing was just outstanding. Crowds of sixty and seventy limited out with four to ten pound walleyes. The only trouble I had was keeping those guys legal. We had a large fish box in the stern that held about a thousand pounds. At first we let customers bring their own coolers on the boat, but that did not work at all. I was not responsible for them. If they were over the limit, which they were at times, they stole fish out of each other's coolers. Because of this, I had to go to a number system, and had them bring stringers. Some of the stringers had 12 clips; others had 6, and still others had 10 clips. They paid no attention to the limit, so I started to furnish the stringers with 10 clips, because the limit was 10, then. So what did the customers do? They got their limit and kept on fishing. If they caught a bigger fish, they took the smaller dead fish off of the stringer to dump it back into the water. It was a full-time job to keep them honest. I finally set a rule that anyone I caught doing that would be banned from the boat. That measure seemed to slow down the cheating.

We had some great fishing the day that Bud Rizor came down to the boat at the dock at Hot Waters. He came along on an afternoon trip and filmed the action. The movie was sponsored by GM Chevy on a major news channel. The film came out great with clips of: 5, 6, 7, or 8 fish on hot at once, and the crew netting two and three walleyes at a time in one net. We had to stop that because we were breaking nets. Lorain received some fantastic exposure on national TV, and the crowed started coming from everywhere. In some cases, we had some international crowds from Japan, Africa, Italy, Germany, and other countries. They were coming to Lorain to fish on this big, beautiful boat. We were so proud of the boat, and so certain that all of the clubs and businesses in the area would come to support it. We had: Kids' Day, Ladies' Day, Fathers' Day, and Buddies' Day. In one season, we offered a $500.00 prize for the biggest walleye caught off of the boat. That money was won by Dennis, a regular, who did nothing but catch big fish! His winner was 33 inches long, and weighed in at 12.5 pounds.

The *Big Miss* was not without her problems though. On one trip, we averted a bad fire with about forty people on board. We were drift fishing about ten miles out, and I started the port engine. I didn't hear a thing. I thought, at first, when I hit the start button that I heard a noise. I walked slowly down to the engine hatch, so as not to alarm the passengers. I climbed down in the engine room and smelled an electrical burning smell. Then I looked at the starter on the starboard engine, which was fine. As I walked between both engines, I stepped over the port reduction gear and moved back to where I could see the port starter. The heavy starter cable was laying on the engine bed, and it had burned off right at the starter motor. The bare wire was laying about an inch away from the steel engine bed. There was a 32 volt cable straight from the batteries, and if it had hit the engine bed, it would have burned its way completely through the steel resulting in an unstoppable fire.

Later on, I was called out to take some Coast Guard inspectors off of a tanker. There were about twenty guys on a shakedown cruise of a ship just out of the shipyard. I received a call from the yard to go get these guys, and I agreed that I would if I could find a crew. But my crew was nowhere to be found, so I called Captain James, an ex-master and retired Captain of the Coast Guard. I asked him if he would like to take a ride out to see some of his old buddies. He said he would, and came down to the boat. I had been working on my fire hose, which was just above the engine hatch, and had the fitting open, and the hose off.

We ran out to the tanker about three miles out, and laid to, while the crew on the tanker collected their gear in order to leave the ship. The captain was up in the pilot house with me, "BS-ing" about the lake and sailing. As we were laying up there with the engines running, I thought that I heard a strange noise. I told the captain that I was going to check the engine room before we were to pick up the guys. I, no more than got down on the deck, when I heard the noise, which sounded like my fire pump. I turned into our passenger cabin, and good God! The fire pump was on all of this time, and sending water into the engine room. I opened the hatch and just about "crapped!" The water was half way up on the big diesels, and we were on our way to sinking. I jumped down into the water, opened all my bilge lines, and shut off the fire pump outlet to the deck. After that I opened the manifold to the bilge and went up to the pilot house to tell the captain what had happened. At the same time, we were signaled to come along side to pick up the crew from the tanker. Little did they know that they were getting on a sinking boat! Our pumping system worked just great, because the bilge was dry by the time we got to the dock.

Another snafu with the *Big Miss* came when the steering went out, and I had to bring the boat back to the dock, using the engines to steer. Passengers on the boat had no idea that there was any problem. Some did ask why we had to keep running the engines at different speeds, coming in, but I never told them the reason.

Lots of people used to come down to our dock at Hot Waters, just to see me turn the boat around to dock. The slip was about ninety feet wide, while *The Majestic* was seventy-two feet long. The engines had power to spare, so I spun the boat around using that power. It was impressive for them, but it really didn't require that much training. The boat handled great. I used to tell everyone, "The dents are in the Navy boats!" Life was great, and we were having a ball!

In September of 1984, I decided to take the *Miss Majestic* back down to Key Largo for the winter. I had my nephew, Jim Stringfellow, my dad, my mother, and my wife, Virginia, make the trip with me. By September 21st, we loaded all of our food and clothing aboard. I also loaded 4 fifty-five gallon drums of fuel aboard, plus we had the fuel tanks topped off at 600 gallons. The extra fuel was insurance between fuel docks. We lashed the fuel drums to the bar on the after deck. I wasn't really happy about doing that, because, if and when we encountered any heavy weather, those drums could be a hazard if they broke loose. Anyway, we got underway and set a course for Port Colborne, the entrance to the Welland Canal. The next morning we arrived there, and I bought fuel again, just to make sure we had enough on board. Some fuel docks can be few and far between, and I didn't want to take any chances, so I fueled up every chance we had.

We spent the day locking through the locks and laid over until morning to get underway. We started out at 6:00 am, and set a course for Oswego, New York, the entrance to the Oswego Canal. We arrived at the Oswego Marina at 6:00 pm, tied up at a dock, and made a call to the dock master to lock through the locks on the next morning. We could have gone right into the lock system, but I had to take the mast down from the pilot house, so that I could clear the bridges. We entered the next morning, cleared the lock, entered the canal through Lake Oneida, and tied up at an amusement park nearby. We walked up to a restaurant, ate breakfast, and got underway. Before we left the dock, however, we found that we had a stowaway. A cat had come aboard, and we almost took him to Florida. Some child would have been missing his pet, so we put him ashore. We ran all day until we came to the Erie Canal and entered the locking system—up, up, then down, down, down, until we got to Troy, New York, and entered the Hudson River. We stopped at a small marina, and went in to take a shower and to wash up. It was cold outside, and there was no heat in the shower. The water was lukewarm, so we didn't spend too much time in the shower. We were tired out, and hit the sack. After getting underway at 6:00 am, we had about 150 miles to run to New York City. I discovered that I had a bad vibration in my port engine. Coming out of one of those locks, I must have hit something and didn't realize it until now. When I came up to speed, I damaged a prop. I shut down the port engine and ran on one engine, which cut our speed down to 8 knots.

I don't recall how long it took us to get to Peterson's Marina at Nyack, just short of New York City, but we docked there and met an old timer, who just loved to talk. He informed us that they used to build PT boats there, and he didn't miss a beat explaining the details. I was hoping the marina had a lift there to haul *The Majestic* out, but they did not, so we took on fuel and got underway for Cape May, New Jersey. We stopped at another small marina near Bayonne, to see if they would haul us out and repair our prop. There was a lift, and as they were about to haul us out, I became kind of apprehensive about hauling here. There didn't seem to be any repair shop around, and this was out in the boondocks, so to speak. I just had them put her back in the water, and we got underway with one engine. I could have used the port engine, if I had to, but to save any further damage, I just ran on the starboard engine.

We passed under the George Washington Bridge, passed the Statue of Liberty, and ran out into the Atlantic Ocean. By this time, it was dark, and we were off the New Jersey coast about ten miles out. We listened to all kinds of chatter on the radio, "Mayday, need help, on fire, and sinking." The Coast Guard was soon at the scene. We suddenly came up on a bunch of running lights, which I determined was a bunch of shrimpers, who were trawling. We zigzagged through the shrimp boats and finally cleared them. We passed Atlantic City, and the sky was starting to lighten up. We spotted the sea buoy at Cape May and entered the channel. We ran up past the Coast Guard station and docked at Point Aphino Marina. I used both engines to dock. We spotted a little restaurant, after we checked in with the dock master, and headed for some breakfast. When we returned, the boat was hauled out, and the mechanics had started to work on the prop. That is when I found out that the shaft was also bent. At 4 pm, all work stopped, and the workmen went home. They informed us that they may have to cut the shaft coupling off and get a new shaft made. They were not able to get the coupling off, even after they tried to use a hydraulic puller. After they left me, my nephew and I went down to the engine room and started to work on getting that coupling off. It was 2:00 am by the time we were successful, and went to bed.

The next morning we heard that a hurricane was to hit Cape May, later that afternoon. I rented a motel room and returned to the boat which was high and dry on blocks. I informed my parents about the hurricane and told them that they should go up to the motel. They refused and wanted to stay on the boat. My nephew, Jimmy, also said that he was happy right where he was, so my wife and I went to the motel to shower up and to go to bed. At 10:00 pm, the wind and rain hit—blowing at gale force and pouring down rain. I got up, dressed, and went down to the boat. As I climbed up the ladder, I was just about blown away. When I entered the cabin, my mom and dad were sitting there, playing cards. They asked me what was the matter, and I replied, "Oh, I was just wondering how you guys were."

The next day, the crew returned to work and was surprised to see the coupling off. They removed the shaft and took it up to a repair shop. The day after, they had the shaft straightened and installed along with the prop, as well as put the boat back in the water. It was late, so we stayed over another day. That next morning, we were laying at the dock, and I was down in the engine room checking it out. Suddenly, my wife just got up and walked through the cabin into the after part of the deck. She fell through the hatch that I had left open—about a six foot drop. As she fell, I tried to catch her, but it happened so fast that I was able only to slow down her fall. We got her out of the engine room, onto the deck, and called an ambulance, which took her to the hospital. The x-rays showed that she had a badly sprained ankle. Thank God that it was not broken!

When we returned to the boat, we found that the marina was socked in with fog. When I checked the radar out, it worked fine. I went into the office and paid for the repairs, which came to $1,800. We cast off the lines and away we went with both engines working. The radar picked up the channel, and we got out into the ocean, underway to Norfolk, Virginia. The sun came out; the fog cleared, and it was a beautiful day. We noticed lots of debris from the hurricane in the water as we proceeded on to Norfolk.

The trip was uneventful until we got near Norfolk. It was midnight, and I noticed that a port running light was out, so we tried to get a new bulb in, but it still did not work. I reported the incident to the Coast Guard, just in case. I picked up the channel markers for Norfolk Harbor on the radar, and we entered the shipping channel. As we neared the inter-channel, I heard a bunch of hollering voices down below. I looked out to the bow deck and saw my mother and father standing with their hands raised and a guy pointing a gun at them. My heart felt as though it was going to jump out of my chest as another guy came running up the ladder to the pilot house! He entered and identified himself as the United States Coast Guard. I was relieved and explained our destination and purpose. He checked my papers and told me that I had my running light out, and they assumed that I was a smuggler. I was happy to see that they were on the ball and told them so. I advised him that we were looking for a marina to lay over, so he directed us to a nice marina, while they escorted us there. We thanked them, and they left.

We docked next to a beautiful 75-foot yacht and went to bed. The next morning as I was lying there half a sleep, I heard an engine start—Crash! Boom! Bang! I jumped out of my sack and ran up topside. There was that 75-foot yacht with her bow way up on the dock. Some young guys had the boat, started the engines, and apparently ran the damn thing straight ahead up on the dock. I did not know what they were trying to do, but whatever it was, they went the wrong way. It was such a sad thing to see such a beautiful boat, like that one, get damaged.

We got underway and were in the Inter-coastal Waterway. It was not too bad at this point, but later on, in Georgia, we ran all day and saw the same type of churches on the shore. We got to a small lock that let us down a foot or two, and then we were done with locks. It was all waterway from there. We worked our way down to South Port and laid over there for the night. The next morning we headed for Charleston, South Carolina where we docked for that night. When the sun came up, we went back out to sea, but our charts did not show an opening that led through the breakwater and out to the south and over a bar. I had the option of going out the main channel, or running over that bar. I decided on the small opening and headed south toward Jacksonville, Florida. We encountered large sea swells that brought the water depth from eighteen feet down to ten feet. I was not familiar with this area, so I decided to run east to get some better water under me. By this time, the water was beginning to get rough and it was getting dark. I turned on the radar and picked up the main channel markers to return to Charleston, because I did not want to make it into Jacksonville in the dark. I played it safe.

At sun up, it was blowing hard, and the ocean was making buffaloes, so we picked up the Inter-coastal, and headed south. About halfway down Georgia, I ducked out a little channel and went outside to the ocean. We ran to Jacksonville with no problems, where we pulled into a shrimp dock, got fuel and ice. Boy, they took a large hose and filled our big cooler to the tope, and the fuel price was about $1.10 a gallon. When we got underway, it was eighty degrees out, so we stripped to our shorts and enjoyed a beautiful trip down to St. Augustine. After docking, we spent the night in such a beautiful city. The next day, after fueling up again, we headed for Miami. It felt good to be outside running again! We passed Cape Canaveral. It was so beautiful to run day and night in such calm, warm weather. My Loran went out about half way down the Florida coast, so I had to run "Course and Time." At 1:00 am, I saw a tanker running up behind me, so I called him on the radio to ask for my position, just to double check my reckonings. He informed me that I was off Port St. Lucie.

By morning we were in the Palm Beach area, where the ocean was calm, but a thunder storm was up ahead. The wind picked up and blew hard. The ocean gets white caps, but no big sea. We were running in the Gulf Stream, and our speed dropped. We continued down the coast, passing beaches, beaches, and more beaches, until we finally sighted Fort Lauderdale Channel. I talked with a bunch of charter boats and asked where to dock. They asked me if I was lost, and I said no, but maybe they could direct me to Pier 66 Marina. It was a fantastic spot with phone service, hookup, newspaper in the morning, and a great restaurant. I decided the next day to run the Inter-coastal to Miami, which was an interesting trip past every conceivable home and boat. We passed my old fishing spot at Haulover Docks when we used to stay at Miami Beach. It felt a little funny going past there on my own head boat, when I used to go out on the head boats there. I remembered the riptide in that channel, because I had to use lots of power to keep steerage.

After clearing the Haulover Channel, we headed down the Inter-coastal to Key Largo, which had me a little worried. The marker buoys were far apart, and if visibility was not good, it can be kind of "hairy." The water was so clear and so shallow that it was hard to make out the channel, but Jim, my mate, did a great job of picking up the markers and keeping me in good water. I decided that if I ever did this again, that I would run outside where it is faster and safer. We ran past shoals that I had fished before out of Key Largo. I saw the large towers that were near Howard Johnson's restaurant at Key Largo. Later on, I saw Molasses Light, the tower for Molasses Reef. I was in familiar waters! I took up the heading and ran the channel into Key Largo. Anyone who has ever entered this port can tell you that there is no room for error. Boats of all shapes and sizes were docked on both sides of this channel and it cannot be much wider than sixty feet across. There were some good-sized boats running out of there! This was my first time running this channel, and I made it right up to the Holiday Inn Dock with no problems. The *Miss Majestic* was home again. We had covered more than 1900 miles in three weeks. Everyone on the channel was hollering, "Welcome home, *Majestic*." It was a great trip, but now I had to get set up to start running fishing trips again, and that's another story.

In the spring of 1985, I had to go down to Florida to bring the *Miss Majestic* back to Lorain from Key Largo. I asked Chuck Plato, my son-in-law, Mike Pozega, and my son, Bob, to come along to help me make the trip home. We all caught a flight to Miami and took a bus down to Key Largo.

The weather was great when we got underway. The ocean was calm, and it was eighty-five degrees out. The weather was just great for our trip. We sailed up the Florida coast and into Jacksonville with no problems. The warm sunshine made this trip fun. My crew trawled a fishing line as we went, and we boated some barracuda on the way.

We ran the ocean all of the way up to South Port where we encountered a problem with the port engine, shutting it down, and running the last one hundred miles on one engine.

We entered South Port and docked at a marina on the Inter-coastal Waterway. My crew went over to a small restaurant, while I went down into the engine room to check out my port engine. I soon found out that the main water circulating pump on the engine was leaking badly at the seal, which explained the heating-up problem. When my crew returned, we began to remove the circulating pump to get it repaired. I checked with the marina, and they informed me that they could have a new seal put in at the Detroit Marine dealer there. We got the pump out and took it to be repaired. My engines were built with a reservoir that lets oil drippings collect under the engine so that they don't go into the bilge. The older 12v-71 engine was a great engine, and a real workhorse, but it was dirty, and most dripped oil. We generally just pumped the oily water into a bucket and took it ashore to dispose of it in a waste oil drum. Because we had lost so much water into this sump, there was little we could do with all of that oily water, so we got some oil emulsion soap and dumped it under the engine to clean it up. I put a weight on the float to keep it from pumping, until we had the pump back, and installed. We were then going to get underway, run out into the ocean a ways, and pump the oily water overboard, but it really did not look too bad. As an aside, a pint of oil in the water looks like fifty gallons when pumped out of a boat. There wasn't much else we could do, because it was late at night by then, so we decided to wait to get underway until the morning. We hit the sack, and when daylight broke, I went to the marina to pay our bill. As I walked back, I saw a film of oil in the marina, which wasn't bad, but it was there! I ran back to the boat, jumped down into the engine room, and sure enough the water and oil were gone. The float had somehow popped loose and pumped the bilge dry. I woke my crew and told them to hurry and get dressed. "We gotta get outa here," I yelled. After we left, I spent half of that day looking over my shoulder for the Coast Guard to stop us. As luck would have it, we never did hear anything on it! The tide was running out that night, and it carried most of the oil away. That is one thing that I am normally very careful about—oil from bilge water. I even installed sensors in my bilge pump's float that would not pump oil, but pumped water only. Back then, in the 1980s, the pollution situation was not as serious as it is today, and oil in the marinas was a common thing, but I never got used to it. As harbormaster, I had lots of trouble with it. After we got home, I received a letter from the marina thanking us for stopping and it was looking forward to our return, so I guess they had no problem with the oil.

We ran the intercoastals all of the way up to Albemarle Sound, but the weather had turned bad, and we encountered wind gusts of up to ninety miles per hour. There was a tornado warning in the area. Just as we approached a narrow channel coming out of the open water of the sound, a severe thunderstorm hit, and visibility went to zero with the wind and rain. My wind gauge showed on the peg that the wind speed was up to 100 miles per hour. White caps made the bay invisible, and my radar was a blank. I spun the *Majestic* around to retrace my course out into the open water. My crew went nuts because they wanted to get back into the river. I told them in no short order to shut up and to sit down. I wanted water to maneuver, not some narrow channel to run aground.

As most thunderstorms do, the wind quit, and the sun came out, so we continued on our way.

That night we anchored in tidewater near a small island. The sky had clouded over, and it was pitch black out. We dropped anchor, and I went back and got some squid out of the bait box. I baited up a pole and threw it out. I heard a noise coming from the engine room, so I set my fishing rod down and opened the engine hatch. Both props were turning, and the engines were off! The tide was so strong that it was turning the props! I closed the hatch and went back to the stern to pick up my rod. My crew, which had already gone to bed, started giving me the raspberries. They said, "What the hell do you think you're going to catch here? Ha! Ha! Ha!" Instantly, my pole bent double. Either I got the bottom or a very big fish! Bob, Mike, and Chuck jumped out of their bunks and were standing forward of the fish box. I was on the stern. I reeled the fish in, and discovered that it was a four-feet-long shark. I got him up on deck, and tossed him over the bar. Three guys headed for the hills, screaming. I laughed my ass off! Before the night was over, we must have caught twenty sharks of all sizes. When the sun arose, we pulled anchor and were underway. I noticed an empty beer can that was on the point of the anchor. Those sharks had been drinking beer!

Our trip from this point up to Norfolk was uneventful until we hit Chesapeake, Virginia. We pulled in and noticed the channel was full of boats docked on both sides. We found out that the lift bridge was broken and would take a week to repair. It didn't bother me too much as I had nowhere to go but home, but my crew wanted to leave. I called my wife and asked her to fly down, to bring my nephew, Jim, and to meet me there in Chesapeake.

She did, and Mike and my son flew home. I had a new crew: my wife, my nephew, and Chuck. At least with her on board, we would eat some decent meals!

Finally the bridge was repaired, and we got underway, stopping in Norfolk to fuel up and to get some groceries. As we cleared the outer channel buoy, I set a course for New York. The wind picked up out of the northeast. Shortly, it was blowing 25 miles per hour, with gusts up to 30. The sea was building, so I decided to return to Norfolk. We were twenty-five miles out, but I felt that it was not a good idea to stay on course, and I played it safe. By the time we returned to Norfolk, the wind had picked up to 40 miles per hour with gusts up to 50. As I turned to head up the channel to enter Norfolk, the wind was on my beam, and the sea was beating the hell out of my starboard side. We began to roll, and I became worried about the fuel drums that we had lashed to the bar. I tried to put the wind on my starboard bow as much as I could to kind of tack to slow down the beating that we were taking. I gripped the wheel so hard that my hands hurt, because the expanse of the bay was not hitting us broadside. I then saw a wall of water about a half mile away coming at me. I could not, for the life of me, figure out what it was. I discovered that it was an atomic submarine coming down the channel, heading out to sea. I saw his wake for a mile behind him. We finally got into some protected water and made for the marina. I was assigned to a dock that was broadside to the wind, and it was blowing a gale. There was a beautiful million dollar yacht downwind from my dock. With little or no room to maneuver to get turned to enter the dock, I noticed some brand new, newly treated pilings in the marina. They were big poles aligning each dock. I knew that if I didn't carry good speed into my turn, the wind would get me, and I would be paying some billionaire for damages to his boat. I came into the entrance of my slip, underway at a good clip, swung the boat broadside to the wind, and let the piling catch my stern. I entered the slip, and all was great until the piling snapped off. I missed the yacht by inches, but got to my dock. We laid over for the night and left the next day, stopping at Cape May. We spent a day or two there, then went up to New York, took a picture of the Statue of Liberty, and continued on to Nyack, where we fueled up. The next day it was up the Hudson River, over to Troy, then up and down over mountains through the New York Barge Canal to Oswego, New York. We traveled back across Lake Ontario to the Welland Canal to Lake Erie, and home. It was the last trip for this great little boat, which we kept and ran charters until 1999, when we sold the boat to the Starlight Fleet in Cape May, New Jersey.

**Statue of Liberty—Picture taken as I Entered
New York Harbor**

Miss Majestic at the Dock in the Marina

Miss Majestic Entering Lorain Harbor from Key Largo Trip

My Wife, Virginia, with Three Nice Perch

**Two Boards Full of walleye and Steelhead
Caught by Dayton Crew**

CHAPTER 9 - LITTLE MISS

FISHING IS MUCH MORE THAN FISH, IT IS THE GREAT OCCASION WHEN WE MAY
RETURN TO THE FINE SIMPLICITY OF OUR FOREFATHERS.

HERBERT HOOVER

Things were going really well with the *Miss Majestic*; and my son, Bob, had gotten his Coast Guard Master's papers, so we flew down to Miami to see Raleigh Stapleton, the owner of Stapleton Boat Building. We sat down with him to iron out a deal to build us a 41 foot Stapleton Boat with twin v-6 92 GM engines. The boat was to be built with USCG specs and certified for passengers for hire. This is the type of boat that my son and I went fishing on when we were down in Fort Myers, visiting my parents. We were really impressed with the boat and decided to get one built. We had it constructed so that fishermen could have access to the bow and have lots of cabin space to get in or out of the weather. I bought the engines from a firm in Baltimore. As I said before, they were two 6-v 92 turbo GM diesels with 400 horsepower each. I don't recall now just how long it took have the boat built, but we looked forward to the boat getting to Lorain, so that we could complete it. The deck house and flying bridge had to be removed and shipped separately, so that when we got the boat, we had to install the hydraulic steering, the anchor winch, bolt the deck house down, install the flying bridge, install railings all around the boat, hook up the wire ring, and build seating and bunks up forward, plus install a "head."

We rented a heated stall inside of my friend's building at Bob Vanwagnen's Marina on the East Side. We worked on the boat for about a month for eight to ten hours a day to get it ready for the water in March. We took it down the hill at Bob's place in Sheffield, and launched it in the Black River. We started the engines for the first time, and ran it over to 9th Street and docked it at Armco Company Dock. Ted, the owner, a great guy, let us dock there to finish the boat.

Next we had to get the boat certified for passengers, which included getting the boat stability tested. The Coast Guard does this by putting weight on the boat in different places to see just how much the boat lays over, so they can determine how many people to all us to carry. I went up to Builders' Supply Company, and they let me use 50 pound bags of salt. The Coast Guard had us put the bags aboard, and they ran the test, and arrived at 37 passengers that this boat could haul safely. We had to buy forty life jackets and a life raft, plus an "EPIRP," Emergency Position

Indicator that sends out a signal to the Coast Guard so that it can find a specific boat, if it sinks. After all the tests and equipment, we had to take the boat out to demonstrate retrieval of an overboard passenger, plus anchor to see that all systems were running correctly. We finally got our papers and were cleared to take passengers.

We took the *Little Miss* over to the dock, next to the *Miss Majestic*. The next day, I told my son that we were going to take the new boat out for a shakedown run and to bring it to full speed, and run some tests ourselves, before taking on passengers. We got underway, ran out past the lighthouse, and brought the engines up to speed. Everything seemed to be running fine, but when I went to turn around, she kept going straight ahead. No matter where we turned the wheel, she did not respond, so on our first trip out, I had to bring her back to the dock, using the engines to steer. Once there, I shut the engines down, and we began to check out the steering. I opened the after hatch, and there in the bilge was a puddle of oil. The nut on the hydraulic oil line had never been tightened. All we had to do was to bleed the line, add oil, and we were back in business.

We started to run trips on the boat, and my son was doing a great job with the new boat. We had customers from all over coming down to ride on this sharp boat! We had a party that wanted to go up to fish Kelly Island Shoals, so Bob agreed to take the party there. His boat ran about twenty miles an hour, and they got up to Kelly's and fish. The lake had a wind blowing about 15 or 20 miles per hour. The *Little Miss* was supposed to return at about 2:00 pm. I was down at the dock with the radio on. I was just about to call my son to see where he was, when all of the sudden, I heard him holler over the radio for me to get up to the pilot house, and turn on the radio. My son informed me that his boat was sinking. I asked his position, and he said that he was about ten minutes from the lighthouse. Chuck Plato, my crewman, was on the dock, so I hollered for him to get the lines loose, and we got underway. We neared the lighthouse, just as the *Little Miss* was rounding it. I pulled along side and took off all of the passengers. Bob was still underway, and he beached the boat on the sandbar inside of the breakwater. He had opened the bilge pump manifold, and was pumping water out of the engine room. The water was halfway up the side of the engines. A hose clamp had broken and let the water enter the bilge. After about fifteen minutes, he had it pumped out and was back to the dock. The Coast Guard came down to investigate the issue, and later commended us on how we handled the situation.

One spring, we took the *Little Miss* up to Port Clinton to run trips out of Brand's Marina. We had been invited there and ran trips with no problems, until we suddenly noticed a change in the way we were treated. Some of the smaller charters "cried" about this beautiful boat stealing their customers. The diesel fuel pump suspiciously was broken, or the fuel price had doubled, and we could see that our welcome had worn out. We left there, and never went back. Later I tried to get a dock up there for the *Big Miss*, and was just about to close the deal, when the local charters found out. All at once the deal was dead in the water, so to speak! I never could understand that either. We could have really brought big business to that area, and all would have prospered, but little minds prevailed.

We ran the *Little Miss* until 1997, when we sold it to a firm in St. Petersburg, Florida. I hated to see it go! We lost about $50,000 on the sale of the boat, but the port engine had all but driven us nuts! One thing after another went sour. At one point, Bob started the port engine; it turned over and then went clunk! Water had entered the cylinder head, and broke a piston. Another time while he was running, the port reduction gear blew up. We had to shut down operations to replace the gear. I hated to see the *Little Miss* come! Every time, it was "Hey Dad, that port engine . . ." These were newly rebuilt engines, but what could I do, when the builder is in Baltimore, and I am here in Lorain, so I bit the bullet!

After I sold the *Little Miss*, I wanted another boat for my son to run. My wife and I were going on vacation in Florida, and so we would stop to take a look at a boat in Savannah, Georgia. We drove down and met with the owner of a 31-foot Tiara that was for sale. He took us down to the marina there, and as we walked out on the dock, he stopped at a fantastic, beautiful boat, and said, "There she is!" The boat looked to be brand new, with all of the seats covered with canvas. The boat had a beautiful pipe tower, and a full canvas cover over the cockpit. He uncovered it to reveal a fantastic-looking inside, with a 17-inch-fish-finder, all kinds of electronics, 110 generator, air, heat, full controls, and the tower. Inside was filled with white leather seats, which seemed to be brand new. I fell in love with the boat, and we asked to take a ride. The owner got in and tried to get the hydraulic hatch open. It did not do so right away, and it took him twenty minutes to get it open. He tried to start the engine, but it was no good; it wouldn't start. He started the starboard engine, and it sputtered to a stop. He then informed me that he had not run the boat all summer. After some time, he finally got the engines running. Off we went in the open water, where he cranked the engines up to speed. We went about five miles an hour, and left a four-foot-wide wake behind us. I looked at him and asked, "What in the hell do you have here?" He responded that he was going to pull the boat out of the water to check the props. We ran over to the marina to pull the boat out. Once she was ashore, we saw the problem. The props and all of the underwater gear were covered with barnacles. We sat there while all of the barnacles were cleaned off by hand with a scraper. After an hour, we got back into the boat, ran out, and he cranked her up again. She ran right up to 30 miles an hour, and looked very good. At once, the port engine stopped, and the smell of gas engulfed the boat. By this time, I was sick, and told the owner to dock. We went back, and I left without making an offer.

On our way to Key Largo, we stopped at Fort Lauderdale at a marina to look for a boat. I talked with a broker who informed me that he had a 30 foot Rampage Twin Diesel for sale. We went down to look at it, and she looked great! After the engines were started, we were to run out in the ocean, but the water was very rough. I ran the boat and stopped it to let it drift. She handled the sea great, so I offered $60,000. We finished our vacation, and the boat arrived in Lorain, just about the same time as we did. It was spring, and we ran the boat all year. It was a fast boat, but no one wanted to work on her engines. They were a type of GM engines that mechanics don't like, so the following year, we sold this boat to a guy from Long Island. We had to get another boat for my son for the next spring

That winter I started to look for another boat in a marine paper that advertises boats for sale. I came across a 31-foot Tiara, a 1988 model with twin 350 horsepower gas engines. The boat was in Punta Gorda, Florida. We had just bought a new Buick, so we decided to drive down to look at this boat. Our trip down was great until we got to Florida. The state was on fire! As we neared Punta Gorda, the smoke was so thick that the traffic was stopped, and we waited in the car until fire trucks and fire crew got to the area. It had been dry, and the fire had consumed large tracts of timber and dry grass. We finally got to our destination and looked up the boat's owner. We found the address and approached what we believed to be a $600,000 home on a canal.

When we got out of the car, we were met by a short, little guy who had no personality at all, and he was all business. He walked us around the house to the backyard that was spacious, and beyond that was the Tiara, sitting in the water. It was a neat-looking boat with a half tower, and it was clean! I asked if we could go for a ride, and he grunted. I asked again, and he agreed. Virginia and I got into the boat with his wife, who had come out to look us over, and him. He started the engines, which sounded great! We left the dock and went out of a little jetty into the gulf. The water was calm, so I asked him to crank it up to speed. He pushed the throttles wide open to a speed of about 15 miles per hour. The engines were screaming, but we went nowhere.

I told him, "Man, you got a problem with your props!" He just looked at me like what the hell do you know about my boat. I got half pissed off with him because we traveled all of the way down here, and the boat was not running well. Plus, he and his wife treated us like scum. I told him to take us back to the dock, that I was not interested. I think that made him think twice. He said, "If you and your wife will allow me, I would like to take the boat over to the marina, pull it out, and check the bottom." I was in no hurry to drive home, so we took the boat over to the marina which was a scroungy-looking place with 200 cats running around. The lift looked like it was built in 1870. The owners of the place slowly got around to lifting the boat out of the water. As soon as it cleared the water, we discovered that both props were tangled with large pieces of rope. The Tiara owner then said to his wife, "Oh! Ya remember when we had that big rope get caught in the prop?" They cleared the rope from the props and put the boat back in the water. Afterwards, we went back out in the gulf, and when he opened her up this time, she ran great. I gave him a check for $66,000, and we signed the papers and made arrangements to ship it home by truck.

That spring, we set the boat up for charters, and soon found out that there was not much money in a 6-passenger boat. We sold the boat in the winter to a local sport fisherman in our marina, and we were again looking for another boat. This time, I wanted another head boat. I needed a boat before spring. We heard of a 30-foot Island Hopper for sale in Sarasota, Florida during that winter. Again, we were off to Florida to see yet another boat. Again, we encountered a large fire that was burning trees and fields. The smoke made it hard to breathe, and it blanketed a large area of the state.

When we arrived in Sarasota, the smoke was still detectable. We found the owner of the Island Hopper, and he took us down to look at it, which turned out to be a 1997 model and was in very nice shape. It was 30 feet long and had a 12-foot beam. We took it for a ride, and it ran great. I checked out the engine, which was a Caterpillar, Model 3116 turbo cat that had 300 horsepower. It was set up to haul crab pots and had a large hydraulic pump and puller. We dickered about the price, and I offered $50,000. He turned it down, so I asked what he wanted for it. His answer was $75,000. I told him to forget it and started to walk away. He told me to make another offer. I said, "Take off your hydraulic lifter, etc," and offered $60,000. He said to make it $66,000, and the boat was mine. I bought the boat. I had him take the boat over to a marina to pull it out and get it ready to ship to Ohio. I made sure that he understood that the boat had to be winterized. The craft arrived in February, and we cleaned it up and got it ready for a Coast Guard inspection.

First, I had to buy a life raft, and then we had to put a stainless steel railing all around the cockpit, and an EPIRB. We also had to purchase an emergency engine shut down system to comply with the Coast Guard regulations for passengers for hire law. When we finished with the boat, the Coast Guard came down to the dock and put the boat through a stability test, and checked out all systems. It was certified for 15 passengers.

We ran this *Little Miss* for two years before my son, who was her captain, came down with a malady caused by Agent Orange. He was unable to talk and underwent an operation on his throat which took twelve hours. He was hospitalized for over a week, and his days of being a captain were over!

Now I had two boats and no captain. As much as I hated to, I sold the *Little Miss*. It was a toss up as to which boat to keep: the Tiara or the Island Hopper? I was sorry that I chose the Island Hopper, because its factory had gone out of business, and this type of boat was now worth $100,000. I sold mine for $55,000, and it was immaculate! We are now down to one boat, the 31 foot-Tiara.

This year's fishing has been outstanding with walleye limits every trip. The Island Hopper was the best sea boat that I have ever had. As you read earlier, there have been a lot of them.

Lake Erie has been a fantastic body of water over the years. It has survived some traumatic changes, yet is resourceful enough to come out of them, and to produce more fish than all of the Great Lakes, put together. I have been blessed to be born next to this outstanding fish-making machine. If and when I meet my Maker, I will thank Him for this great treasure that so many have enjoyed so much. Gotta go fishing!

My 42-ft Stapleton, *Little Miss #1*, with Passengers

Little Miss 2, a 30-ft Rampage

Boat renamed the *Little Miss #3*, a 31-ft Tiara

Little Miss 4, a 36-ft J-C

Little Miss #5, a 30-ft Island Hopper—Great Boat!

**My Son, Bob, and me at the Cleveland Sport Show-
The Guy in the Middle Is our Crew**

CHAPTER 10
BIG MISS PROBLEMS

GOOD THINGS HAPPEN TO
THOSE WHO BAIT

AUTHOR UNKNOWN

My daughter, Carol who was born in 1958, was now helping with the business and working at the telephone company. The boat was doing okay at this point, but lacked the kind of promotion to bring it to the level it deserved. We were taking river and lake cruises at $5.00 per person. The excursion went up the Black River to the steel plant, then out into the lake, to Lake View Park. It lasted about one and a half hours, during which I narrated highlights of the area, which people just loved. Lorain Metro Parks organization worked with us, bussing people down to the boat. We docked the boat at the north end of Oberlin Avenue at Hot Waters. We were doing great with people coming down by the hundreds, just to see what we had caught and when we took fishing trips out. Our fishing charters lasted from 8 am to 1 pm, and we charged $15.00. The walleye fishing in the 80s was fantastic. Limiting for 50 guys was an everyday event. The mayor at that time, worked along with us and was a great help in getting us started. Later on, another mayor did his damnedest to keep the boat in Lorain. He was a great guy and worked hard to make us feel like we were wanted. The bait store at Hot Waters was doing a fantastic business, because people were coming from all over the country and from other countries to see and to ride on our boat. We were putting Lorain on the map! National television filmed a fishing movie, produced by Bud Rizor, a noted promoter at that time. We, the *Majestic*, were featured on the show, called "Head Boat Heaven." Literally thousands saw the show. Things were beginning to fall into place because we were making money, and the boat was bringing people and business to Lorain. The city was behind us; the Port Authority was behind us, and the public was happy. Sport fishermen were having a ball!

Then one day, the roof fell in. We had a trip scheduled with the Chamber of Commerce, which was to be a river and lake cruise. On the day of the trip, there was a member of the Chamber, standing at the gangway of the boat, signing in people who had a reservation. A prominent guy and his wife walked up to the gangway to board the boat. The guy with the clipboard stopped them, telling the couple that they were not allowed on the boat without an invitation. I was watching as they started to walk away. I went over to the guy at the gangway and told him, "That couple is Mr. so and so, and his wife. They were VIPs here in Lorain. Can't you let them on?" He became very nasty with me, and said, "No way! Only invited guests are allowed." From then on, there were complaints—that we were using the dock free, and we were a hazard to navigation, that we were using up all of the parking. The VIP, we heard through the rumor mill, told the bait store owner, "I will get that boat and that guy out of Lorain, if it takes all the money in my checking account."

Next, a councilman came after me because of the harbormaster job. A policeman wanted the harbor job. That councilman went nuts that I had a bigger boat than he had. A member of the Port Authority also wanted the harbormaster job. The politicians did all that they could to make life miserable for me and for my family. The newspaper picked it up, and it made great copy for the jealous waterfront bums, plus it was just what the bitches and complainers wanted—to get me fired as harbormaster. There was a City

Council hearing on the matter. In attendance was a guy, who was head of the small boat harbor group and who was paying practically nothing to rent a whole marina for 75 boats, got up and began shooting his mouth off about me having free dockage at Hot Waters. Look who was calling the kettle black! I did not believe my ears! A lawyer, rolling in dough and has a free marina, was blasting me! The Battle of Lake Erie was on again! Where was Admiral Perry when I needed him?

This situation reminded me of the trouble I had with the commercial fishing business in the 60s, 70s and early 80s. We had fought with some over fishing rights, so our tugs were vandalized, dock lines were cut, nets were ruined, and we were constantly harassed by the ODNR, because it sided with the sports fishermen. While I was home one night, a friend called, and asked," Is this the harbormaster?" When I identified myself, he went on, "We were down at the lake on the East Side and saw some guys in a small boat stealing fish out of some commercial nets." I grabbed my gun and headed for the boat. My son had a fast outboard at that time, so we ran down to the East Side in the dark. When we approached a boat near the nets, it took off and began to get away. We gave chase, and I yelled for the thieves to stop. I fired a warning shot in the air, and they stopped. As we neared the boat, the guys started throwing fish overboard. I told them to follow us, which they did and we turned them over to the police.

Day in and day out, this was the kind of life I had to live, so I finally sold the fishing tugs and bought *The Miss Majestic*, thinking that the "worm would turn," and we could relax and make a living without trouble. But, it was soon apparent that the jealous bastards were still at it. One promise was true; they were not going to stop until I was out of business or worse—dead!

But, after we were humiliated in the paper and by the City Council, we were told to move to the new marina being built on the East Side. We took the boat over there, but there was only one short dock, just long enough for the *Majestic*. We docked there and had to start our advertising all over again. Where the place was being built, there was very little parking for our customers. Early on there, we had a wedding party come down to the boat for a wedding, and members fell in the mud that covered the parking lot. I had to wash them off with a hose. This was the kind of support that we were getting from Lorain, now.

I bought the boat for Lorain—I live here! We purchased this boat for a lot of money, and paid a high rate of interest. Our payments were $2,500 per month. Soon after the move to the new marina, we were approached by a marina in Port Clinton that wanted us to bring the boat there. They promised to do all of our advertising and ticket sales, if we agreed to move the boat. We had become successful in Lorain with trips to McGarvey's Restaurant in Vermilion, cruises to ball games and river rides. As I said before, I bought the boat for Lorain—I live here. I did not want to take my boat anywhere else. Just when we thought we had endured as much hardship as we were able to here in Lorain, the Port Authority dumped us in favor of an out-of-town boat. I had an offer from Cape May, New Jersey, who wanted to buy the *Majestic*. I declined the offer. I bought another boat, the *Little Miss*, for my son to run, and he was doing a great job. Between the two boats we had lots of people coming to Lorain in the peak vacation months of June and July. It was in the other months that we needed help to make our investment pay off. It did not happen. One day we came down to the dock and discovered that the *Miss Majestic's* dock lines had been cut again. People left human feces in front of our gate to the boat. Our brochures were scattered all over the dock. I went to see the mayor to see if he could do something for us. He refused to see me and my wife. Another time, a later mayor had the Jet Express come in for the Chamber of Commerce to take a ride. He came down to the marina and told it to move the piece of junk, *Majestic*, so the Jet Express could park there. I moved it, as a favor to my friends at Jet Express, not for the mayor. Again, this was the kind of hardship that we had to endure. He further humiliated us, when we invited state senators and dignitaries to ride free, ending the trip with a dinner at Riverside Park. That mayor came down to the park and asked, "What in the hell are you guys doing on that garbage scow?" It may have been funny to them, but it wasn't to us. We were proud of the *Majestic*, and we had a real interest in making Lorain a tourist attraction. Another boat came into Lorain, later, and tried to make a go of passenger service, but gave up after one season. Our efforts to keep the boat here were starting to wear me down. After being active in the Port Authority, I was now being ignored. My letters to the Port Authority on various issues were not being answered. I was an outcast, because I wanted to see the *Majestic* succeed, while others hoped to see us fail. As a result, I called the mayor and said, "I have a chance to sell the boat. How do you feel about that?" All I wanted was, "Oh, my God, don't sell it; we need that boat." Well do you know what his answer was? "Make an appointment with my secretary, and we will talk about it." The next day, I called the Starlight Fleet in New Jersey and sold the *Majestic*. A few months later, I wrote to the newspaper and explained some of Lorain's shortfalls, and the reason that I sold the *Majestic*. True to this town's image, the editor came back with, "You're just a whiner; Lorain doesn't need any whiners." It makes me laugh. When an important member of our town or society comes out and makes any remarks, it is constructive criticism, but when "Joe Blow" says something to make a point, it is whining. Lorain lost a chance to have a much bigger cruise ship here because that was my plan, but after this situation, I didn't need the aggravation.

CHAPTER 11
REFLECTIONS
THERE IS CERTAINLY SOMETHING IN FISHING THAT TENDS TO PRODUCE A GENTLENESS OF SPIRIT, A PURE SERENITY OF MIND

WASHINGTON IRVING

My son, Bobby, as a 9-year-old survived pneumonia, and the normal bumps and bruises of a young boy, growing up. I spent a lot of my spare time playing baseball with him. Virginia and I went out to Lakeview Park to hit balls to him, and he became interested in baseball. One day we were at Lakeview and a guy, named Jim McCartney, came up to us and asked if our son would like to join his team. He and Bob Parker managed a ball team in the Hot Stove League, named the Medics. McCartney had Bobby throw a few pitches, and without another word, signed him up as a pitcher. I told Bobby, "For every guy you strike out, I will pay you 50 cents." Well, to make a long story short, I had to bring that 50 cents down to 10 cents, sooner than I thought. Bob turned out to be an outstanding pitcher all the way through high school, and after. He pitched his team to a state championship, and later ended up pitching for the Barry Buick Team in Cleveland Class-A Ball. Bob was a good-looking kid at 6 feet, 2 inches tall with a good arm. He had a great chance of making the pros, but the Vietnam War had started, and most young guys were enlisting in the Army. Bob decided to join the Army, and ended up in training at Fort Knox, Kentucky. After his basic training, he was assigned to the First Air Cavalry and sent to Vietnam. He became a radio operator and was involved in some major conflicts over there. One of the more enlightening aspects of the story was a phone call from Bob over in Vietnam. He informed us that he had been on a pass from the action and had wrestled a bear and won a donkey. He wanted to ship it home to us. We told him no, in no uncertain terms, to keep the donkey. He later told us that the donkey died and that the major made him dig a hole to bury it. Later, he was wounded and awarded the Purple Heart. When he was med-evacuated to Japan, he met up with a Japanese girl and wanted to ship her home to us. We about "crapped!" No! No! No! She later phoned and cussed us out, saying, "You people are sombitchy."

He was blown off of a bunker and injured his right shoulder, which ended his pitching days. Not only that, but he had been sprayed with the foliage killer, Agent Orange, as planes flew over and dumped out the stuff. After the war, he received his Captain's papers and was running charters with his boat, the

Little Miss. As fate would have it, he ended up losing his license due to the complications from Agent Orange. He began to experience labored breathing and ended up in the VA hospital to have his throat operated on and a hole in his trachea to breathe. The operation took twelve hours. Since then, he has been in and out of the hospital and recuperated to a point where he can communicate through a voice tube. Now he drives us nuts talking, because, for a long time, he could only whisper. He and his daughter have bought a farm house in Berlin Heights, Ohio, where he is happy raising chickens, pheasants, and mastiff dogs.

When my daughter was born, and I saw her for the first time, I told my wife that the nurses must have gotten the babies mixed up, that she was not ours. She had coal black hair, dark skin, and looked like she had a big nose. When my wife took her in bed with her at the hospital, she used to squeeze Carol's nose as if she could have changed it! Ha! As time went on, we saw that we had a most beautiful daughter, and she turned out to be a great gal! Growing up, she used to play with notepads, listing all kinds of entries and billings. After high school, Carol wanted to become an airline stewardess, but flying worried us. We let her make up her own mind about what she eventually wanted to do.

She completed an application from the phone company as a switchboard operator. Over the years, she worked hard, and the company realized that she was a dedicated employee. She worked her way through the ranks to eventually be in charge of the Great Lakes Area as a professional in charge of selling phone services. Now she is flying all over the place.

It is now the year, 2007. The *Majestic* was sold in 1999. My son's boat, the *Little Miss*, was sold, and we are now down to one boat, the 31 foot, Skipper Two. As I look back at the past 25 years, I reflect on how fast these years have passed. My God, my kids are now 50 years old, and my wife and I are great-grand parents.

I have lots of good friends in the charter business and enjoy the chance to meet people and to share the enjoyment of taking out small groups of 6 people or less to fish in this wonderful Great Lakes resource, Lake Erie. I have never lost the thrill of getting up every morning to go down to the dock and to see that beautiful morning sun come up, to smell the early morning air, as we prepare to go out fishing. Although my wife's health has failed over the past ten years, she still enjoys the perch fishing and has become my best buddy. I now spend lots of time on my computer which is something I really enjoy. I now share my thoughts with people all over the world. When I first bought my computer, my wife and daughter told me that I would never learn to operate that damned thing. "Why did you spend your money on that?" They forgot that in recent years the navigation equipment on most of the boats that I ran was computerized, so I adapted to the computer very easily. When I first started to run tugs, there was no radar, no GPS, and no Loran—just a compass. Navigation was by course and time.

As I reflect back on my time in the Navy, I remember most of the great guys that I had the opportunity to serve with, and I still contact the skipper of the destroyer that I sailed. His name is Otto Schirni, a tall, Italian guy who is now living in Fort Lauderdale, Florida. He is 96 years old, and retired from the Navy as an admiral. Like the old saying, "Old sailors never die, they just fade away. Well, I guess that's right, as I have lived a great life with no regrets. My family has been blessed by God, and they, for the most part are happy, healthy, and still alive.

I miss the commercial fishing life, and the *Miss Majestic*, but I now also realize that my body is starting tell me to slow down, that I have nothing to prove. I have sailed the seven seas. I have flown the skies, and dove to the depths of the oceans, all over a period of 80 years. I have seen presidents come and go. I met and served with a president's son, who was a great guy whom I learned to love and to respect. My close friend is an admiral. What else could a kid from Lorain, Ohio, who started out sailing a borrowed comet sailboat want? To top that off, I was the harbormaster. I was proud to have had the chance to serve the citizens of Lorain in that job. I wish that I could have done more to make them proud of me, but it was not to be. God Bless this great country of ours, and may it always remain free!

*   *   *

As I close this last chapter of this book, I am devastated by the death of my wife, Virginia Jaycox. Her death at the Cleveland Clinic has this family in shock. She had been experiencing serious health problems, but the doctors gave us a great report on the outcome of her recent operation to repair some damage. Later complications led to her death. My sixty years with her as my wife were an exciting and loving experience. She was the mother of two grown children: a son—Bob and a daughter—Carol, who have enriched our lives with grandchildren—Nicole, Lisa, Joanne, and Christy. We also have five great-grandchildren.

Our hearts are broken. Virginia was a fantastic woman who constantly worried about others. Words cannot express my personal loss. As a couple, we were one; if you saw her, you saw me. We laughed together, played together, and hurt together. She was my buddy, my friend, and my love. It is only fitting that she loved angels. Our house is filled with angels. Those who met her, loved her. She never, never spoke badly about anyone, and always, always loved to meet new people. On many occasions, she was recognized by others from our years with the Miss Majestic party boat. Dinny, as we called her, often sold the tickets and went along on the boat. She is now in heaven with her mother and father, her brothers and sisters, as well as my mother and father. She, later in life, became close to my mother, and now rests beside her in her grave. My house has an empty feeling, just as my heart does. The years in the future will be very difficult without her, but the memories will live on forever. Thank you, God, for letting me share my life with this beautiful woman. May God bless her soul and may she remain forever in my heart.

Bob, not Capt., not RA, just Bob.

Skipper-2 at the Dock in the Marina

Skipper-2 in Lake Erie Fishing for Walleyes

Sunset on Lake Erie

The Love of My Life—My Best Fishing Buddy

MY BOATS, BOATS, BOATS

Rowboat
Comet-class sailboat
U. S. Mayrant
Ding Dong
Satan's Waitin'
Horace Johnson
Betty J. I
Betty J. II
Betty J. III
Ronald E.
Mermaid
Miss Majestic
Little Miss I
Little Miss II
Little Miss III
Little Miss IV
Little Miss V
Skipper 2

EPILOGUE

A COLLECTION OF
ARTICLES AND PICTURES

The Commercial Fisherman

Day will break and he'll awake. His favorite fish
aren't there to take.

His arms are weary, his back is sore. His love
of the Lake he cant ignore

His catches are few and his pay is small
his loved by some and hated by all

The day of the fisherman has come and past
He'll sail tomorrow and fish till the last

The blue sky above the sea at his side
His love of life cant be denied

They poisoned his Lake and cut up his nets
Hard work is his life and he never forgets

So as you look down your nose at that old tired face
Remember he's human and hard to replace

When he's gone from this Earth you'll then realize
Who catches the fish for your weekly fish fries.

Capt R. A. Jaycox

This article was printed in the *Ohio Magazine* in July 1986, and was written by Sue Gorisek, which was retyped *in toto* in order to avoid the advertisements that were part of the magazine, and so that it would fit in the format of this book.

OHIOANS: THE NET LOSS AND THE BOTTOM LINE

When Bob Jaycox was a little boy, barely able to walk, he'd sneak down to the lake, in defiance of his father, whose spankings scarcely deterred him. The *water* was all he cared about—the way it looked and smelled and felt. Later, he saved $6 from his paper route for an old kayak and a gallon of paint. He was in such a hurry he didn't wait for the paint to dry. He set off, vaguely in the direction of Canada. Late that night, when he finally came home, with streaks of paint on the seat of his pants, his father spanked him again. But Bob was unrepentant.

"You'll never keep me off the water," he howled.

Bob is 60 now, defiant as ever, and loyal. He loved Lake Erie when nobody else did: in the 1950s, in the polio scare, when people said Lake Erie was infectious; later that decade, when the mayflies disappeared, and people said Lake Erie was dead; in the 1970s, when the other commercial fishermen gave up, unwilling to fight a tightening net of restrictive laws, Jaycox wouldn't give up, he'd been on the water too long. He was racing sailboats at fifteen, on a Navy destroyer at seventeen, on a lake freighter at twenty-one. When he grew tired of traveling, he bought a fishing tug and went into business for himself, with his new bride at his side.

It was unglamorous work, but satisfying even on cold March mornings when they'd get a jump on the season by breaking through the harbor ice to head for open water. Virginia stood ten hours a day, working the nets, her galoshes gripping the ice deck, as she dodged the poisonous spines of the catfish that often came up with the perch. Sometimes snow piled up at her feet, as deep as the fish. Once, the lake froze around them, and they were locked in an ice jam, fifteen miles out, in a howling wind, praying for a thaw. Fishing was brutal business, made more so by cutthroat competitors, mean-tempered waters, and drunken sailors. Bob figured he had trained 500 crewmen in the thirty-five years he fished on Lake Erie. Often they worked a month and disappeared, usually with the police in hot pursuit.

Bob never drank, and he kept a tough kind of order on his boats. The older sailors grew to respect him—for his knowledge and his hard work—until, eventually, Jaycox was an old sailor himself. But, by that time, everything had changed.

The sport fishermen's lobby had gotten a law passed that put gillnetters like Jaycox out of business. He was bitter, but not defeated. If he could not have Lake Erie on his terms, he'd have it on theirs. What's more, they would pay for the privilege of keeping him on the water.

Now, on a good day, when Jaycox's twice-daily fishing charters are running fully booked, 156 fishermen pay him $15 each to fish from the *Miss Majestic*. Their lust for walleye keeps him where he wants to be.

The *Miss Majestic* is a splendid boat, a 72-foot, twin-diesel craft that was built by the Miami Yachting Company for a customer who changed his mind when he heard the price: $450,000. Lorain had not seen such a grand boat in years. When Jaycox first tied up, at the foot of Broadway, the waterfront loungers hooted and predicted bankruptcy. At the time, there were no fishing charters operating out of Lorain. But Jaycox knew there were big walleye there. He had been watching them all his life. All he had to do was to prove he could find them.

The first weekend that the *Majestic* sailed with a charter, he returned with 200 good-sized walleye. The customers were pleased, and the waterfront loungers were more than respectful. Some conceded that the Captain might have a chance.

"Where's *Mama Majestic?*" the boaters ask one another, knowing that when Jaycox has a good day, chances are, they will, too. He leads them way out, where they've not fished before, and they follow like ducklings in a row, nearly to the Canadian border, where the water is 55 feet deep and the big fish swim lazily, out of reach of the conventional fishermen who tend to stay much closer to shore. Out here, the walleye can be as big as

16 pounds and 36 inches long. Some are twenty years old, and the fishermen say they are shrewd grandpas, too *smart* to have been fooled by a worm.

Most days at noon, Virginia Jaycox waits on the pier, watching for signs, as sailors' wives do. If it has been a good trip, the *Majestic* will come in flying a black-and-green flag that signifies all the fishermen have caught their limit—six fish apiece. Virginia always hopes to see the flag. When the *Majestic* has a bad day, the fishermen are sullen and Jaycox is nervous. It goes beyond a reluctance to disappoint his paying customers. On a bad day, when the fish won't bite, they seem to make a liar of him.

Jaycox never bought the official line, that commercial fishermen had depleted the walleye. He was familiar with the statistics, promulgated by the Ohio Department of Natural Resources, but he never believed them. He saw their statistics as part of a plot—a justification for their doing what they wanted to do. Yet, the numbers are persuasive. According to the ODNR, the walleye population reached its peak in the decade between 1945 and 1955, when commercial harvest ran as high as 6 million pounds a year. With pollution and over-fishing, the numbers declined each year after that. By 1969 the commercial catch was a mere 139,000 pounds. The next year, when traces of mercury were found in the fish, Ohio put the walleye off-limits. Two years later, sport fishermen were permitted to take walleye again, but commercial fishermen were not. In time, the population increased. By 1977 sportsmen were taking 2.2 million walleyes a year, and by 1984, they were catching 4.1 million. Suddenly the walleye meant big business to the hard-pressed little towns on the shore. Last year the sport fishing industry generated nearly $1 billion in economic benefits to communities along the lake. An influential sport fishing lobby began to win friends in Columbus. During the years of debate the statistics seemed beyond argument, but Bob Jaycox never stopped arguing. Even now, with the battle ended, he is still arguing, with a dogged logic colored by wishful thinking.

"There's plenty of fish for all of us," he says. "The experts just don't know where to look."

Since he *did* know where to look, Bob figured he could earn his living by selling his knowledge. Virginia thought it was a good plan, too, until she saw the size of the *Miss Majestic*—and the size of the mortgage payments.

"Two thousand dollars a month, at our age," she cried. They were in their middle fifties and had talked of retiring.

Virginia also worried about the Captain's ability to tolerate a daily association with hook-and-line fishermen. He'd always considered them woefully ignorant in the ways of fish, and he doubted they loved the lake as much as he did. He could be infuriatingly condescending. He said that sports fishermen were poor slobs who worked at jobs they hated, while they wished they could be on the lake every day as he was. He said it was envy that motivated his fight to put the gillnetters out of business. In the old days, on the tugs, there was no need for diplomacy. But now he'd be forced to tone down his belligerence, and Virginia wasn't sure that he could. She knew he had a long memory for old grudges.

The battle of Lake Erie had been a bitter and protracted fight, with casualties on both sides. There was gunfire on the waterfront those years with a frequency that hadn't been heard since Prohibition, when rumrunners like to shoot one another out of the water.

The shootings in this fight were more in the nature of malicious mischief—shot-out tires and the like—but there were skirmishes nearly every day in the summer. Often when Jaycox went out to deep water to retrieve his nets, he'd discover that someone had cut them loose from their buoys, leaving them to sink to the bottom, where they could not be recovered. Of course, the netted fish all died at the bottom, but in the fight over walleye, the combatants had forgotten about the *fish*.

The morning Jaycox found his tug cut loose and its windows smashed, he began carrying a shotgun. Some of his surlier sailors were out for blood, and there was one near-drowning. It happened when a young game warden got into a brawl with a hot-headed crewman, who had been a prizefighter in his younger days. They were rolling around on the deck when the sailor leaped to his feet, yowling that the warden had bitten his ear. He avenged himself by hurling the warden overboard, jumping in on top of him and holding his head under until the bubbles stopped. Jaycox separated them just in time.

A dozen armed game wardens were dispatched to the hazardous duty of the waterfront to enforce the detested walleye ban. They never found any illegal fish, but they did find a set with too fine a mesh, which they confiscated. Jaycox paid a $100 fine, and the loss of the net cost him another $1,000. He felt persecuted, surrounded by enemies: wardens who pulled his nets by day, vandals who pulled raids at night. Eventually, the cost of the fines, and the escalating violence, discouraged all but the most stubborn gillnetters. By 1983, Jaycox was the only one still operating throughout the season between Cleveland and Vermilion. Finally, that spring, the state put him out of his misery. Gillnetting was banned altogether, and Jaycox was compensated for his equipment.

It was a final armistice in a fifteen-year war, and to Jaycox, a bitter defeat. For the first time he felt old: fifty-six and nowhere to go. The other old sailors looked for dry-land jobs, but he never considered it. Instead, he did what he always did when he felt blue. He went out to look at boats. In his vulnerable state he was a pushover, and the *Miss Majestic* spoke to him insistently, against all reason. So he bought it and hung out his shingle: Captain Bob, Fishing Charters.

Virginia says that he has mellowed some. He is learning to enjoy the company of the enemy. He carries a fishing pole now and casts out a few times to be companionable when they are all bobbing together aboard the *Majestic* on the waves far out on the lake. But he soon grows bored with it and puts the pole away. To a man accustomed to hauling in fish by the ton, taking them one at a time is no great thrill.

On Lake Erie some things never change. Each year in October the boats are befriended by flocks of wild canaries in their southward migration. They perch on the rails and fly about in the pilothouse, hitching a ride. At the same time, Canada geese trace an irregular V against the sky. To Captain Jaycox, the spectacle of the fall migration is startlingly beautiful, an annual reward for his hard work on the water. In the old days, the sight always moved him. He and Virginia would stop whatever they were doing to watch the birds. Now he must share the spectacle with strangers, but he finds that it's not so b ad, some of them see the beauty in it, too.

Now that peace is restored to Lake Erie, Jaycox is like an old warrior who has seen enough of battles; he won't forget, but he has stopped fighting. One day last summer he telephoned his old adversary, the supervisor of law enforcement at the Ohio Division of Wildlife, to invite him to bring the game wardens to Lorain for a day of fishing on the *Majestic.*

"My treat," he said.

The gesture was tantamount to surrender, and some might see it as the ultimate humiliation. But not Captain Jaycox. He is like Admiral Perry in victory. He has met the enemy, and they are his.—SUE GORISEK

News Release for the Lorain Charter Boat Service Retyped in Its Entirety to Fit the Book's Format.

FOR RELEASE AS DESIRED

MAJESTIC VOYAGE A ONCE IN A LIFETIME ADVENTURE FOR SKIPPER

(Lorain, Ohio)—Beginning in April, 1983, the 72-foot charter boat Miss Majestic starts its first full year of commercial operations on Lake Erie out of the Port of Lorain. Fishing and family adventures await all who discover this "largest and fastest" vessel of its type on the lake.

Regular runs out of this fresh water port, however, exciting themselves, would never have been possible without the adventure of Captain Robert Jaycox, who commanded the voyage of Miss Majestic from its previous salt water home in Key Largo, Florida, to the Lorain harbor in August, 1982.

Skipper Jaycox turned a 35-year career as a commercial fisherman on Lake Erie into a new way to celebrate his long friendship with the lake waters, when he decided to purchase the Majestic ("It was love at first sight.") and undertook a 13-day cruise up the Atlantic coast, through the Welland Canal and into the Port of Lorain to be escorted by U. S. Coast Guard as a Lorain fire truck sprayed a welcome and bridge operators sounded horns of approval.

The journey of the Miss Majestic was chronicled by Captain Jaycox in the captain's log. It was originally published in the *Lorain Journal* and is reprinted here with the *Journal's* permission.

The Journey of the Miss Majestic

Sunday, Aug. 1, 1982

6 a.m.—Left Key Largo dock, wind southeast 15. Set course for Jacksonville harbor, speed 12 knots.

6:55 a.m.—Entered Gulf Stream, beautiful blue water 300 to 500 feet deep.

9:37 a.m.—Passed Key Biscayne. Weather clear and hot, 95 degrees. Stripped down to our shorts. Engines drone on creating an ever-endless tempo.

10:55 a.m.—The endless rows of Miami Beach hotels and motels pass slowly by as we make our course northward: 1,987 miles to Ohio.

Evening—Daylight passes and darkness surrounds the tiny ship. The moon sparkles on the water. The night is beautiful.

10:55 p.m.—The lights at the Cape Canaveral Space Station appear on the horizon 10 miles out from our perch on this little piece of plastic, small in comparison to the vastness of the Atlantic Ocean.

Monday, Aug. 2

4:15 a.m.—Daytona Beach

8 a.m.—St. Augustine. The lights come and go as we take four-hour watches steering and plotting courses. Daylight arrives off St. Augustine and the sun prepares to bake our northern hides.

11 a.m.—St. John's entrance to Jacksonville, slowly comes into view, 646 gallons of fuel is taken aboard along with 600 pounds of ice.

Noon—Left Jupiter Inlet. Back out into the Atlantic. Set course for Charleston, South Carolina.

Tuesday, Aug. 3

4 a.m.—Anchored outside harbor and waited for daylight.

7 a.m.—Entered port. Took on fuel, 320 gallons Reminisced about my Navy days during World War II when the destroyer I was on came into Charleston harbor to get damages repaired at the Charleston Navy yard. The battleship gray of the ships brought back many memories. Leaving Charleston, we proceed to sea, having lost the tail wind of the gulf stream. Making 11 knots, but with more fuel consumption.

11:20 a.m.—On course for Morehead City and the intercoastal waterway. Approaching some of the more trying points of our trip. We are now faced with a decision. Weather has been good so far, but ahead lies a large reef; we will navigate at night. This reef, known as the Frying Pan Shoal, sticks out 25 miles into the ocean and marks a point off Cape Fear. The name alone makes me wish I had studied harder in navigation school.

11 p.m.—We spot the outer buoy off Frying Pan Shoal. The weather was worsened and my main concern now is the safety of the vessel particularly with four 50-gallon drums of fuel lashed on deck to give us the necessary range to travel the ocean route between points. Drums breaking loose on deck could spell disaster. Rain is now starting to fall as a thunderstorm approaches. Visibility falls and, as we approach the reef, larger swells of waves came up on our bow. It was an eerie feeling to watch the depth recorder and know what lay in our path. The depth slowly rises from 90 feet to 32 feet. There is always that unresting at night in bad weather. Spray is now drifting past the pilot house 12 feet above the water and we are now approaching the northern side of the reef and open water.

Wednesday, Aug. 4

12:10 a.m.—Clear of Frying Pan Reef or shoal as they refer to it on the chart. Now we can relax somewhat as we set a course for Morehead City.

5:30 a.m.—the lights of Morehead City now come into view, but we fail to locate the entrance channel light as we pour over our calculations and retrace our navigations. We determine we are approximately one mile south of our desired destination. Running north one mile, we locate the channel and enter the arbor at 6 a.m.

6 a.m.—We notice now we are losing oil on both engines and the starboard red-gear has lost oil. Closer inspection shows a hydraulic hose leak on the gear and an oil hose leak on the engines. Adding oil as we go, we decide to replace the hydraulic hose and repair the other leaks. We are soon in the intercoastal waterway around the Cape Hatteras area. The fuel drums on deck have made me decide not to chance the nighttime trip around the cape. Anyone who has been up the intercoastal can attest to the endless bays, channels and canals that form this chain in the waterway system. It's a little boring but a much safer route. Staying over night at a small marina on the north, we rest, and chart our next leg of the trip. Another 640 gallons of the fuel and we are on our way.

Thursday, Aug. 5

We enter the Norfolk area. Ships of all shapes and sizes are now coming from all angles as we dock at a marina, fuel up and work on our engine problem.

4 p.m.—We are all finished and decide to stay over night.

Friday, Aug. 6

6 a.m.—Under way and proceeding to sea. Passed nuclear sub.

8 a.m.—Set course for New York City

11:30 a.m.—Approximately 60 miles north of Norfolk, 10 miles out. Weather fair, slight swell. Wind southwest, 15. After taking 24 pictures with my Minolta, I discover no film in the camera. Too busy concentrating on my little ship to notice before. Missed some great shots of navy ships. Nuclear sub passed by port side real close with just tower visible. Looked strange to an old navy vet.

7 p.m.—Running all day. Weather beginning to worsen as a cold front moves south. The wind now to the northeast and I am surprised at how fast the ocean has built up a nine-foot sea.

8 p.m.—Approaching the Delaware Bay area. Currents are now working against the northeast wind and the seas have begun to make our ship labor badly. We have now reduced speed to eight knots and must make a decision to go on to New York (eight hours away) or make for Cape May, N.J. It's decided we'll go into Cape May.

9:30 p.m.—The lights of Cape May are visible. Passing the harbor entrance, we decide we have no chart of this port's harbor. Rolling badly now. It's hard to locate the buoys hiding behind the lights of the beach. Slowly we make our way into the small but beautiful little harbor. Not wishing to press our luck, we dock at the first dock we see. It just happened to be a U. S. Coast Guard dock. After being told very politely to move on, we were given docking facilities further in side the harbor. Finally coming to rest alongside a marine railway haulout dock, we secured the boat and ran for the restaurant. After devouring pancakes and bacon, we caved in our bunks at 1:30 a.m.

Saturday, Aug. 6

6 a.m.—After a quick coffee at the restaurant, we are under way, proceeding to New York City and the Hudson River. Wind still east-northeast. Large dead sea still running current and cross seas make the trip uncomfortable, up one sea, down another, pound and rock as the hours go by. Wildwood, Atlantic City, and the New Jersey coast pass by our port side. Realize then that the end of the ocean part of our trip is only four hours away. We have mixed feelings about sighting the New York skyline. Our 72-foot party boat, the Miss Majestic, is on her way to a new life, hauling people on Lake Erie. The fiberglass hull, always used to the warm tropical sea, will now be subjected to the icy blasts of northern winters. I wonder if this little boat will appreciate what I've done to her life.

The big 12v 71 Detroits keep their endless drone as we pass Sandy Hook and make our new course north for New York. Channel 16 on the V. H. F. marine radio is now a jumble of distress calls to the U. S. Coast Guard. One boat overturned, another sinking, and still a third with a fire aboard. Yachts and small craft of all descriptions now dart across our path. Some honor our right-of-way of marine's rules of the road but most ignore it and cross in our path. The New York skyline now is in our view.

Sunday, Aug. 8

5 p.m.—Seven days from Key Largo, we pass the New York entrance buoy, Ambrose Light. We endlessly meet large vessel traffic. First is the large passenger liner, Atlantic. I'd have to write a book to include all the ships we pass as we traverse under the Narrows Bridge. The wind has picked up and large swells follow our stern.

6:25 p.m.—We approach the Statue of Liberty and the Manhattan waterfront. Entering the Hudson River, we head upriver past shipping warehouses. The George Washington Bridge comes into view at this point, 400-foot and 500-foot cliffs on the west bank are beautiful. Stopped for fuel at a quaint old marine supply store named Peterson's Marina Supply. A fine old gentleman met us and delivered some yarns about the old days on the river. Seems navy patrol craft were built there during WW2, Underway again by 10 p.m.

11:45 p.m.—Passed West Point Military Academy.

Monday, Aug. 9

1:30 a.m.—Troy Lock No. 2. Passing through locking system now and vessel is raised about 34 feet at each lock as we approach Schenectady, N.Y., we notice a small change in the vessel's handling. We realize it could be the change from salt water to fresh. Passed Schenectady and many small towns as we go from lock to lock. We are now approaching lock No. 13. It's 2:55 A.M. Monday.

Tuesday, Aug. 10

Underway from lock no. 20. Some experience going over mountains with a boat.

4:40 p.m.—Oswego, N.Y. Wind 25 to 30 NW. May have to lay over and wait to calm.

Wednesday, Aug. 11

Wind still flowing 25 northwest. Lake Ontario rough, 8—to 10-foot seas. Laying at dock, plan to get underway at 6 p.m.

6 p.m.—Under way. Lake rough. Wind NW seas 6 feet. Running for Port Welland and the entrance to the Welland Canal. Making 15 knots.

Thursday, Aug. 12

6 a.m.—Port Welland Canal. Entered Lock No. 1 and proceeded up the Welland. Looks very impressive, five hours to travel the eight locks and stop at fuel dock to take on 540 gallons fuel. Walk into town and end up with a pocket full of Canadian change. The town, Port Colburn, is a quaint little port with the usual clean Canadian appearance

6 p.m.—Under way for Cleveland, Ohio, a 12-hour run

Friday, Aug. 13

6 a.m.—Stopped at Capt. Frank's Restaurant, Cleveland.

9:30 a.m.—Entered Lorain Harbor, the end to a voyage and the start of a new life and career for my wife, my family, and my ship.

Capt. Robert Jaycox

This article is retyped in its entirety and is taken from *The Buzz*, a supplement to *The Lorain Journal*, July 13, 2007, written by Theresa Neuhoff.

Long before Robert Jaycox became "Captain Bob," he was a young teenage boy tagging along with his grandfather who took him everywhere.

It was the trips on Lake Erie that Jaycox remembers most.

Just after the Depression in the early 1940s, Jaycox's grandfather was a bootlegger who took alcohol to the fishing tugs and traded it for fish. It was then that Jaycox became acclimated to the water and grew to love Lake Erie.

"I thought my grandfather was the greatest guy in the world," Jaycox said. "If it wasn't for him, I may not be doing what I'm doing today.

"Fishing gets in your blood. You fall in love with it and it's a lifelong thing. You can't get away from it. If they took me down to Arizona, I'd die."

Jaycox, 81, opened one of the first fishing charters in Lorain. To this day, he is still well known for his boat the "Miss Majestic," a 72-foot drift boat that he owned for 20 years. During the 1980s, walleye catches of 900 pounds a day became the norm on his boat. People from all over the world chartered Miss Majestic, which held up to 80 people.

"It was a mixed bag of people," Jaycox said. "We had people from China and even a soccer team from Japan. It was interesting."

When McGarvey's was still opened in Vermilion, Jaycox offered trips on Friday nights from Lorain for $17 that included a steak dinner.

In 1999, Jaycox made the difficult decision to sell the boat. It has been renamed "Cape May Lady" and is docked in Cape May, New Jersey.

He was still left with two boats: "The Little Miss" and "The Skipper II." For several years, Jaycox's son Robert Jr. chartered the Little Miss, which was a smaller version of Miss Majestic. Jaycox worked until he was forced to retire because of health reasons.

Jaycox sold Little Miss and maintained his charter business on The Skipper II, which is a 31-foot Tiara with twin Volvo diesel engines. For the cost of $450, six people can charter Jaycox's boat for an eight-hour trip.

"The fishing fleet in Lorain doesn't get the notoriety it deserves," Jaycox said. "We have the best fishing right here in Lorain. I've had close to 20 charters so far this summer and we limit every day. It's beautiful fishing."

Over the past few years, the limit of 30 fish per person is common year around on Jaycox's charters. Walleye fishing begins in March in Port Clinton. It moves to Lorain when the water gets warmer in the middle of May and lasts until November. Perch fishing is prime in late summer and early fall.

"I never get tired of fishing," Jaycox said. "I'm 81 years and I can't wait to wake up in the morning early enough to see the sun come up."

Jaycox and Virginia, his wife of 60 years, may catch many fish, but they don't often eat it. They give most of it away and prefer to order fish dinners at the Slovak Club.

When he's not on the water, Jaycox is usually working on his boat that is docked at Spitzer Marina in Lorain. For 20 years, he worked as a Harbor Master for the City of Lorain. His other marine jobs include commercial fishing, commercial diving and commercial towing business.

The lifelong Lorain resident joined the Navy in 1943 and served on the U. S. Navy Destroyer for three years. After earning an honorable discharge in 1947, he sailed on the Horace Johnson, a U. S. Steel ore boat.

Over his lifetime, he's gathered hundreds of stories. For years, his friends and family often told him to put his memories on paper. Finally, he gave in and wrote a book last winter. It is currently being published and will be on the market this fall.

The name of the book is "The Bosin's Pipe." It's an autobiographical book about Jaycox's life on the water.

"I've owned 20 different boats in my lifetime and I've enjoyed everyone of them, he said.

For more information on the Majestic Fishing Charters, go to www.greatlakes.org or call (440) 244-2621.

The charter is one of four in Lorain that is included under the Ohio Charter listings (which can be accessed by using the above web site). The others are R-Boat Charters (David Kastl, 440-282-7023), Y-Knot Charters (Frank Kittrick, 800-473-1748) and Magic Moments Fishing Charters (Bo Rhodes, 800-270-9823).

Other local charters listed include Mega Bites Charters in Vermilion (Tony Denslow, 888-930-9932) and Ritz Charters in Huron (Don Ritznhalter, 419-433-5602).

My Virginia, My Wife, My Buddy

THIS IS DEDICATED TO THE ONE I LOVE